41.49

LEWIS M. KILLIAN, Professor of Sociology at the Florida State University, is a native of Georgia and received his A.B. and M.A. degrees at the University of Georgia. He received his Ph.D. from the University of Chicago in 1949. He taught at the University of Oklahoma from 1949 to 1952 and since then he has been teaching at the Florida State University.

He is co-author with Ralph Turner of *Collective Behavior* (Prentice-Hall, 1956). In 1954 he directed research for the Attorney General of Florida in connection with the Amicus Curiae brief of the State of Florida in the school desegregation cases. Among his published articles are: "The Effects of Southern White Workers on Race Relations in Northern Plants"; "The Adjustment of Southern White Workers to Northern Urban Norms"; "The Purge of an Agitator"; and "Leadership in the Desegregation Crisis: An Institutional Analysis."

CHARLES M. GRIGG, Professor of Sociology and Director, Institute for Social Research, Florida State University is a native of Virginia. After five years of service in the Army Air Force during World War II, he completed work for his B.S. Degree at Richmond Professional Institute, College of William and Mary in 1947. He enrolled at the University of North Carolina in 1948 and received his Ph.D. in 1952. He taught at Brown University from 1952 until 1955 and has been at Florida State University since 1955.

His articles include: "Factors Related to the Virginia Vote on Segregation"; "Two-Party Voting in the South: Class Vs. Party Identification"; "The Bi-Racial Committee As a Response to Racial Tensions in Southern Cities"; "Fundamental Principles of Democracy: Basis of Agreement and Disagreement."

# Racial Crisis in America

LEADERSHIP

IN

CONFLICT

**Lewis Killian**
**Charles Grigg**

Prentice-Hall, Inc.  *Englewood Cliffs, N.J.*
A SPECTRUM BOOK

Current printing (last digit):
14  13  12  11  10  9  8  7

*To our wives, Kay and Virginia*
*who have bravely endured with us the risks of inquiry*
*in an area of dangerous thought.*

# Foreword

*Racial Crisis in America* is both timely and useful. It is being published at a moment of unprecedented civil rights activity requiring communication and decision-making where there is often little experience and even fewer guidelines. It is timely, also, in that while the American Negro citizen may not have achieved his goal of "Free by '63" he has at least made significant inroads into the problem. He has established beyond a doubt, first, that his is a determined, persistent drive, representing a genuine grass-roots dissatisfaction with the status quo; second, that the grievances to which Negro citizens are addressing themselves through their protests and demonstrations are very real indeed; and, third, that as a consequence of his efforts the Negro no longer finds himself alone, but has attracted a substantial number of dedicated and influential white citizens who are willing to face realistically the significance of the racial crisis for *all* Americans. For in a climate of direct confrontation it is inevitable that accepted and age-old practices will be challenged.

Where conflict and tension among groups is inevitable, the availability and resourcefulness of leadership becomes both critical and crucial. Herein lies the great practical value of this book at this moment in history. While pure research and the scientific approach are able representations of the academic world, this publication deals with actual situations, involving individual leaders—white as well as Negro—and an assessment of their relationships and values.

The situations described in this book had their settings in southern cities, but this in no way diminishes the book's usefulness for other cities throughout the country. Montgomery and Tuskegee, Alabama, the student sit-ins, the freedom rides, the independence of African nations, and more recently the March on Washington: all have come together to give the Negro a new determination, a new confidence and a new perspective about his destiny and the roles he and his leaders must play in achieving their goal.

vii

This major domestic problem must be resolved not only *for* the Negro, but *with* the Negro. Biracial committees addressed to local problems are no longer effective instruments simply because they exist, nor can they be conceived of as useful machinery to appease or postpone action on the part of the Negro community. Their value, as this book illustrates, will be at the point where they are truly representative of the entire community, when they include both white and Negro citizens who honestly face up to the inevitability of change and focus on making this a constructive, orderly transition.

The alternatives to this are quite clear. Either we help people become constructive, productive consumers, or we resign ourselves to their becoming destructive, chronic dependents. Either we support and communicate with honest, responsible leadership, both white and Negro, or else we create a vacuum in which fanatical and irresponsible leadership will take over.

The future of our communities, our citizens, our country depends on this decision.

Whitney M. Young, Jr.
*Executive Director*
National Urban League

# Preface

We do not expect that this analysis of the racial crisis will be well liked by our readers. It steps on many toes, and it may arouse the ire of both white and Negro Americans, of both segregationists and integrationists. We do hope that the book will be widely read and, above all, carefully read. We have attempted to look at the conflict of white and Negro Americans from the vantage point of each of the significant actors. The test for each reader will be, we hope, "Do the authors accurately portray my position?" and not "Do I like what they say?"

This volume reflects the results of five years of research in one of the greatest laboratories of social change—the South in crisis. The research was modestly financed at the beginning by grants from the Society for the Psychological Study of Social Issues and the Research Council of the Florida State University. The authors are indebted to the Field Foundation and the Rockefeller Foundation for major financial support of the project. We are also grateful to the administration of the Florida State University and the Board of Control for Institutions of Higher Learning in the state of Florida for their dedication to the principle that the scholar must be free to pursue his quest for knowledge in spite of controversy.

We have received invaluable advice and assistance from Dr. John Griffin, Dr. T. Stanton Dietrich, and Dr. Paul Piccard of the Florida State University, Dr. Russell Middleton of the University of Wisconsin, and Dr. James Prothro, of the University of North Carolina. Dr. A. A. Abraham, of the Florida A. and M. University, performed the research on the performance of Negro high school seniors on the Florida Twelfth-Grade test. We are indebted to him for his realistic analysis and his permission to use his results.

The chapter, "Negro Protest Leaders in a Southern Community," is reprinted (with revisions) by permission of the editors from *Social Forces*, Vol. 38, No. 3, March, 1960. Dr. Charles U. Smith, of the Florida A. and M. University, was co-author of the original article. His friendship and his professional insights have been a valuable aid to the authors during the entire period of the research.

The chapter, "The Role of the White Liberal," was originally written for presentation at the Third Annual Conference on Intergroup Relations held at the University of Houston on March 31, 1962. The conference was cosponsored by the Department of Sociology and Anthropology at the University of Houston and the Southwest Regional Anti-Defamation League of B'nai B'rith.

The following students and former students at the Florida State University participated in the research at various stages: Mrs. Kathy Dykes Wishart, Dr. Charles Newton, Mrs. Harriet Howe Simpson, E. W. Guernsey, Mrs. Jennie McIntyre, Butler Horton, William Stacy, and Henry Stewart. Dr. James Williams assisted in the study of the Biracial Committee.

Mrs. Marge Doyle and Mrs. Janie Lawhorn labored long and patiently in typing the manuscript in its many revisions. They are to be commended for maintaining their pleasant dispositions in spite of the vagaries of the authors.

Readers who are acquainted with their works will recognize the pervasive influence of Herbert Blumer and Muzafer Sherif. Their conceptualization of race relations as *group* relations, not the interaction of discrete individuals, has exercised a profound influence on our research and writing. Blumer's concept of "race prejudice as a sense of group position" is central in our analysis. The concept of "the superordinate goal" was borrowed from our good friend and mentor, Muzafer Sherif.

# Contents

## 3. A Biracial Committee as Seen by the Members          58

## 4. Negro Protest Leaders in a Southern Community     81

## 5. The Role of the White Liberal                         91

## 6. Tokenism—Too Little, Too Late                                           105

## 7. The Spectre of Conflict                                                  130

# ONE

# Race Relations:
# An Era of Struggle

Belief in progress is a persistent theme in American social thought. The irrepressible optimism of the American people has burst through the gloom of despair in the midst of depressions, inflation, war, and the threat of nuclear holocaust. This theme of progress has characterized our thinking about race relations no less than other topics of national concern.

The frequency of editorial comment on "the worsening of the desegregation crisis" and the "deterioration of race relations" since 1954 might seem to belie this assertion. Yet much of the editorial analysis of this crisis implies that the desegregation controversy is an unnecessary and unanticipated deviation from a long-term trend of steady improvement in race relations. The declaration, "Everything was fine until the desegregation decision," has been repeated so often that the first half of this century begins to assume the aspect of a Golden Age of racial harmony. But the mythology of progress reaches even farther back into history, so that the Slavery Controversy and the unpleasantness of 1861-1865 are encompassed as minor deviations from a linear, salutary trend. Even amidst the current cries of alarm, the majority of people do not act as if the crisis were a grave one. Many southern communities still display a "business as usual" attitude.

## THE "UPS" AND "DOWNS" OF RACE RELATIONS

Granting the virtue of optimism and the superiority of belief in progress over a philosophy of despair, the history of Negro–white relations in this country does not present a picture of uninterrupted, consistent progress. If we use as our criteria the degree of tension and conflict between the races, and the status of the Negro in the society, we find the course of race relations has been marked by a series of ups and down, with alternating periods of stability and disequilibrium. While the occurrence of crises such as the present one has not meant catastrophe, neither has the resolution of the crises ever been utopian.

The initial misconception characterizing the popular version of history relates to the very beginnings of Negro–white relations. It is standard to mark the beginning of this side of our history with the landing of 20 Negroes at Jamestown in 1619. What is not so generally known is that these Negroes did not enter into the status of slaves. The tradition of slavery did not exist in the English common law as it did in the codes, civil and canonical, of the Spanish and Portuguese colonies. These Negroes acquired the status of indentured servants, a status which was familiar both in England and in the colonies. Low as this status was, it was one that was shared by some whites, and it was one from which a man could rise by his own efforts. Not until 1661 did the Virginia colony give statutory recognition to slavery as a system, and laws governing slavery came even later in other colonies, north and south.[1]

So we may speak of the first half-century of Negro history as a period of "descent into slavery." One Negro in Jamestown symbolizes the plateau to which even a colored indentured servant could rise. One Anthony Johnson, a free Negro, not only held title to land but held other Negroes in bondage. He went into court and won a ruling entitling him to hold one of these servants in bondage for life. Thus, ironically, one of the earliest slaveowners was a Negro.

During the remainder of the colonial period, slavery became firmly established and the free Negro became an anomaly, his lot little better than that of the slave. There was a glimmer of hope for Negroes during the revolutionary period, when the same ideas of freedom and the rights of man that found expression in the Declaration of Independence gave rise to misgivings as to the rectitude of slavery. It was in these times that the nation first experienced the American dilemma that was to plague it from then on. Ben Franklin, Patrick Henry, James Otis, Tom Paine, and George Washington were among those who questioned both the consistency of slavery with democratic ideals and its effect on the spirit of a free society. Thomas Jefferson included in the first draft of the Declaration of Independence a clause condemning George III for waging "cruel war against humanity itself by imposing the slave trade upon the colonies," but it was struck out on the insistence of Georgia and South Carolina.[2]

This was a false sunrise, however. A Negro historian has called the first generation of our national existence the "Dark Ages of Negro History." [3] The invention of the cotton gin and the advance of the Cotton Kingdom into the southwest bound the South to slavery by economic fetters which the key of conscience could not unlock. Their inability to solve the problem of what to do with the freed Negro, either by removing him from American society or by accepting him as a part of it, prevented some white southerners from supporting plans for the manumission of slaves. At the same time the successful slave revolt in Haiti under Toussaint L'Ouverture and abortive insurrections in the South itself aroused in many people the dread of what might occur if vigilance were relaxed.

Part of the mythology of race relations is the theory that, undisturbed by importunate, meddling abolitionists, the South would have gradually and voluntarily abandoned slavery. Just as it is argued that, with a few more years of segregation, the Negro will be ready for desegregation, it has been argued that with a few more years of slavery he would have been better prepared for freedom. With the increasing restiveness of the slaves and their free Negro compatriots, plus the millstone of the investment of slaveholders in Negroes as property, it is difficult to see how the South would have ridded itself of the incubus of slavery without a violent convulsion of some sort. Be that as it may, the period of the Slavery Controversy from 1830 to 1860 was marked neither by amelioration of the plight of the slaves nor by measures designed to fit them for freedom. Laws were passed making manumission more difficult, placing greater restrictions on free Negroes, and discouraging the instruction of slaves in reading. Moreover, during this era the defense of slavery on the grounds of the innate inferiority of the Negro came to full flower. Ironically the first books written in America with the word "sociology" in their titles sought to prove that slavery was not only just but positively beneficial to both whites and Negroes.[4]

From a legal standpoint, never has the Negro's status been lower than it was in the decade just prior to the War Between the States. In the Dred Scott decision of 1857 Chief Justice Taney of the United States Supreme Court said of Negroes,

We think that they are not included, and were not intended to be included, under the word "citizens" in the Constitution, and can therefore claim none of the rights and privileges which that instrument provides for and secures to citizens of the United States.[5]

So what was the position of the Negro population in the social system of the U.S. 100 years ago? After over 200 years of residence in this country, he could exert virtually no power in his own behalf. If he was a slave, he could run away. He might present the plight of his people to white people in the North, as did Frederick Douglass, and enlist their sympathy. But at the beginning of the War Between the States, he could not even bear arms in the fight against slavery. The Negro was an issue, but he was not a citizen, north or south. And it is debatable whether he was even the main issue in the struggle through which he was to be given his freedom and citizenship.

## THE ERA OF ACCOMMODATION

The developments of the decade from 1860 to 1870 do not represent simply a speeding up of a long-term, evolutionary development of race relations and of the Negro's status. They constituted the establishment of a new mode of accommodation. It was only then that the evolution of the status of the Negro as a citizen began. To speak of customs and traditions as stretching back past this period to the days of the founding of our nation is inaccurate. Customs governing the treatment of the Negro not as property but as a second-class citizen, but still as a citizen, had to develop *after* this. They were not merely old customs now resumed, although they were often influenced by the old ways.

There is now ample historical evidence to show that, during the years between 1865 and 1900, what these customs and the status of the Negro were to be was uncertain. Even after the end of Reconstruction in 1875 Negro voting was far more common in the South than it was to be at a later period. White politicians of all parties wooed the Negro vote. Negroes held positions in the federal bureaucracy which they would not hold again until the time of the New Deal. There was less segregation in many areas of contact, such as transportation, than there is today. The authors of *Segregation in Washington,* published in 1948, concluded that there was less segregation in Washington in 1900 than there was in 1946.[6] Often quoted as symbolic of how insecure the tradition of segregation was at the turn of the century is the statement from the Charleston, South Carolina, *News and Courier* in 1898 in reaction to a proposed law requiring segregation in railway cars:

> As we have got on fairly well for a third of a century, including a long period of reconstruction, without such a measure, we can probably get on as well hereafter without it, and certainly so extreme a measure should not be adopted and enforced without added and urgent cause.[7]

The "separate but equal" doctrine enunciated by the U.S. Supreme Court in the famous case of *Plessy v. Ferguson*[8] gave legal support to the new, still embryonic pattern of segregation. A host of state segregation laws was passed in the ten years following this decision and the pattern of segregation became firmly established. At the same time, the Negro sank lower in status, and race relations became tense and often violent. The Atlanta race riot of 1906 symbolizes the violence which characterized the relations of whites and Negroes in the South during this period. Nor was this deterioration confined to the South. The Springfield, Illinois, race riot of 1908, which Willard Walling described as part of the "Race War in the North," was one of the factors that led directly to the formation of the NAACP, with Walling as one of the founders.

It was during this era following the end of Reconstruction, the restoration of white political rule in the South, and the legitimatization of segregation by the Supreme Court that the Negro learned what was to be his place as a citizen in the reunited nation. The issue of slavery was dead; segregation was now to be the issue.

But there was little that Negroes could do about this issue at the time. Indeed, one of their most famous leaders counseled them to accept the pattern, at least for the time being. Booker T. Washington became the symbol of the philosophy of patience and gradualism. He implied that if Negroes proved themselves good "hewers of wood and drawers of water" the whites would reward them with greater economic opportunities and perhaps, eventually, with full equality in society. By and large Negroes in the South did follow this philosophy, although it is questionable whether they did so because they agreed with it or because they could do little else. At the same time,

the philosophy of another leader captured the imagination of countless Negroes, even though they had little power with which to act
upon this philosophy. W. E. B. Dubois argued that the Negro would
not escape from an inferior status by accepting it, as Washington
seemed to suggest. Instead, he contended, Negroes should challenge
both the pattern of segregation and the restriction of Negroes to the
lower levels of the occupational scale. He was the moving spirit of
the NAACP during its formative period.

James M. Dabbs has summed up the two forces operating in
the Negro community during the past 40 years in these words:

> Because of Washington the Negroes have today a stronger eco-
> nomic life and occupy a more important economic position than they
> would have without him. Because of Dubois they have developed a
> political and legal sense and a remarkable power to plead their cause
> within the framework of American law.[9]

Starting from a position of economic underprivilege, educational
inadequacy, and legal impotence, Negro Americans have, indeed, experienced a half-century of remarkable progress. The gap between
white and Negro levels of income and education has been narrowed.
Both north and south, a significant Negro upper class of professional
and business men has developed. Lynchings have virtually disap-
peared. Through litigation instigated by the NAACP and through
migration to the North, the Negro has become a significant factor
at the polls. Even before 1954 the NAACP had breached the wall
of segregation at several points through a long series of successful
court actions. Although the principle of "separate but equal" still
stood, each decision of the Supreme Court made the definition of
"equal" more rigorous.

It would seem, then, that the theme of progress was finally being
realized and that further crises would be averted. Yet less than a
decade after the *Brown* decision[10] and 100 years from the time of
the Civil War the nation is in the midst of another great crisis, with
racial tensions again at a high pitch. The desegregation decision of
the Supreme Court does not suffice as an explanation of this crisis.
It is only a surface cause, a symbol of the conflicting currents which
have been running all the time beneath the smooth surface of progress
and harmony.

Robert E. Park, an acute observer of race relations from 1913 until his death in 1944, was optimistic about the course of Negro–white relations, perhaps because of the improvements he saw in his lifetime. In a concise analysis of changes in race relations in the South he once said:

> Originally race relations in the South could be rather accurately represented by a horizontal line, with all the white folk above and all the Negro folk below. . . . With the development of industrial and professional classes within the Negro race, the distinction between the races tends to assume the form of a vertical line. . . . The result is to develop in every occupational class professional and industrial biracial organizations. . . . The races no longer look up and down; they look across.[11]

We do not know whether Park thought that this vertical line would gradually and quietly fade, bringing an end to this particular race problem, but it obviously has not. Of course, the line has never become nearly vertical, but Park's diagram of parallel social structures with Negroes and whites "looking across" at each other suggests one basis of the present crisis. It is exactly because so many Negroes have risen enough in socioeconomic status to "look across" that they have acquired the power to challenge the existence of the line of segregation. And, as they have risen and the line has turned toward the vertical, the problem of segregation has become more intense. The Negro who, on the basis of income, education, occupation, and life-style, is able to look across at white men of similar station feels most keenly the stigma of being segregated on account of his race. As the proportion of such Negroes increased, both the incentive and the resources for a direct and effective challenge of the principle of segregation grew.

## THE PROBLEM OF COMMUNICATION

Just as progress within the framework of segregation did not make Negroes better satisfied with segregation, neither did it improve communication and understanding between the races. The Negro has always been able to stay in communication with the white man and gain many favors from him, so long as he approached him as a suppliant and as an inferior. But again, as numbers of Negroes rose in socioeconomic status, they became less inclined to communicate in this role. They withdrew more and more into the isolation of the Negro community, leading a life that was completely unknown to most white people. The drift of Negroes into urban centers, impersonal and segregated, facilitated this isolation. So also did their entry into industry and the impersonal social system of the modern factory. The paternalism and the intimacy of race relations on the plantation and in the small town have become steadily less typical and less significant, even in the Deep South. And it was through the impersonal medium of the lawsuit and in the formal setting of the court that the Negro finally issued his challenge to segregation.

## THE END OF ACCOMMODATION

In challenging segregation in these cases the Negro has also brought into being a new era of race relations. A century ago he was *given* his freedom from slavery. In a hundred years he has gained the strength to *demand* his independence of segregation. This does not mean that in the new era race relations are going to be more harmonious, that the Negro's lot will soon become better, or even that segregation will disappear. What the ultimate resolution of the crisis will be is beyond our ken. But the preceding analysis suggests that this era will be one in which neither personal goodwill nor mutual understanding, but impersonal power, will be the most significant factor in race relations.

The intimacy and goodwill which can exist between the races as long as the Negro demonstrates his willingness to "stay in his place" evaporate when, by challenging segregation, he indicates that he is no longer willing to accept this place. There is no indication that more than a minority of white people, either in the South or the North, are yet prepared to extend both friendship and equality to the Negro. Many people in the North agree with the abstract principle of equality because the impersonality and spatial segregation of the metropolis protects them from intimacy with Negroes. They are not so sympathetic to Negroes as they are isolated from them, physically and psychologically. In the South, white people have reassessed, and often withdrawn from, former patterns of intimacy and friendship for the very reason that they are no longer confident that the Negro "knows his place."

The NAACP, the organized spearhead and the legal arm of the

desegregation movement, has been the chief catalyst in these developments. In the book, *With All Deliberate Speed,* Weldon James characterizes the importance of this organization in this manner:

> Arrayed solidly against the organized segregationists, and one of their favorite targets, is the National Association for the Advancement of Colored People, the interracial organization behind nearly every one of the 100-odd school integration suits filed since 1954, the legal victor in most of the decisions, and, before 1955, the motive force behind 36 of 39 Supreme Court decisions affecting long-established racial customs—including, of course, the school desegregation ruling.[12]

Even when the NAACP has not directly exerted the pressure which has led to desegregation, its influence has been felt. The public schools of Louisville, Kentucky, embarked on a program of desegregation without the costly stimulus of a court suit. But the Superintendent of Schools declared:

> I wanted desperately to be ahead of the NAACP. I wanted to have a tentative plan—I knew NAACP would be in very promptly. . . .[13]

Undoubtedly the destruction or neutralizing of this and other protest organizations would do more than any other single thing to set back the desegregation movement. Evidently leaders of the fight to preserve segregation have operated on this assumption. The *Race Relations Law Reporter* summarizes the reaction of southern leaders with the statement:

> State governments throughout the South have drawn on the ingenuity of the past and added their own devices and new combinations of old ones in pressing their counter-attack against the NAACP and other organizations favoring integration of the races.[14]

But attempts to destroy the NAACP have so far proved unsuccessful and it continues to be one of the prime movers in the desegregation process. In the meantime, the principal mode of dealing with it has been through litigation. Nor has it been generally approached as an honorable and legitimate opponent before the bar. It has been accused of barratry, inciting to riot, and collaboration with the Communists. It is hardly surprising that the defenders of segregation

have shown no inclination to communicate with the organization outside the courtroom or the legislative hearing room, in view of the
prevailing definition of its character among white southerners.

## FUNCTIONARIES AND PRESSURE GROUPS

Communicating with Negro leaders in this limited fashion have
been the functionaries, elected or appointed, of state and local govern-
ments. Partly by mandate, partly by default, the task of speaking for
the white South has fallen to them. Herbert Blumer has defined
their position as "pivotal" in the desegregation crisis. He says:

> It is important to recognize that in any given kind of racial seg-
> regation there are strategically placed individuals or small groups
> who set the policies and issue the orders without which the given
> practice of segregation could not be maintained. . . . Thus, control
> of the decisions of the chief functionaries responsible for the actual
> operation of the practice of segregation offers a direct means of
> arresting or immobilizing that practice.[15]

In spite of the increasing incidence of debates between southern
political functionaries over ways to prevent or limit desegregation, it
is still virtually unheard of for one of these key figures to countenance
publicly any degree of desegregation except as an inescapable evil.
Advocacy of "voluntary desegregation," no matter how gradual, is
still suicidal for the public official.

This is not to imply that the NAACP and the political functionaries are the only actors in the situation. Blumer argues that the
pivotal position of the decisions of functionaries makes organizational
pressure and support especially important:

> The carrying through as well as the blocking of deliberate
> desegregation depends on mobilizing and focusing influence and power
> on central functionaries.[16]

While functionaries may act on the basis of their own attitudes,
their intuitive assessment of the state of public opinion, and their
interpretation of election returns, they are keenly sensitive to organizational pressure, which is often the most coherent and easily
interpreted expression of public sentiment between elections. Pro-

segregation "resistance" groups constitute one source of organizational pressure. In 1956 Harold Fleming, of the Southern Regional Council, estimated that at least 20 such groups had appeared on the southern scene since the Supreme Court's 1954 decision.[17] While concluding that their efforts were foredoomed to eventual failure, Fleming assessed their political importance as follows:

> Political control of at least four southern states is in the hands of politicians who are wholly sympathetic with the aims and the methods of the resistance groups. . . . In four additional states, the resistance groups exert strong, if not always decisive, influence on the legislatures and public officials.[18]

Although they can claim only a small minority of the total white population of the South as members, these groups still comprise the largest body of southern whites who are mobilized for the expression of their opinions on the question of desegregation. The opinions they express by words and actions are, of course, unequivocally prosegregation.

In contrast, white southerners who advocate acceptance of desegregation, for whatever reason, are largely unorganized and are only occasionally vocal, and then cautiously so. Yet the organizations that do draw their members from this "silent South," and occasional declarations of opinion by individuals or groups, constitute important evidence of the existence of a "third force" in the situation, in contrast to the openly militant NAACP and the activists of the resistance movement. But what is the nature of this third force?

In 1957 the Southern Regional Council compiled a list of 28 organizations, other than the NAACP, "engaged in human relations activities in the South." [19] A third of these were departments or committees of churches, such as the Christian Life Commission of the Southern Baptist Convention. Negro–white relations constitute only one of the areas of concern of such bodies, and many of these groups lack the full support of the denominations which they represent. Six of the organizations listed were Jewish organizations, not concerned primarily with Negro–white relations and all having national headquarters located outside the South. Two of the groups, including the Urban League, were predominantly Negro organizations; two others were labor groups. Yet another type included such associations as the American Civil Liberties Union, the American Friends Service

Committee, and the YWCA. Such organizations as these have broad concerns in the field of human rights or human relations and vary in the proportion of the total effort they devote to the desegregation crisis.

The only organization that is indigenous to the South, is a "membership association" in the sense of having local branches, and is primarily concerned with the problems of desegregation is the Southern Regional Council itself and its affiliated state and local human relations councils. It is an interracial organization with headquarters in Atlanta and was organized in 1944 as the successor to the Commission on Interracial Cooperation. It includes in its program, in theory or in practice, all of the types of activities utilized by other groups except the legal action characteristic of the NAACP.

These types of activities may be listed as follows:

1. Fact-finding and dissemination.
2. Influencing functionaries.
3. Providing channels of communication.

The most tangible signs of the efforts of these organizations are related to the first type of activity, carrying on research and disseminating the findings. Through its professional staff and consultants the Southern Regional Council carries on a continuous research program, publishing its findings through news releases, books, and its monthly publication, *New South*. In the words of William Peters, in *The Southern Temper*,

> Its information services include a panel of specialists from various fields who serve as consultants to public and private leadership in Southern communities.[20]

It should be remembered, however, that it can provide these services only upon invitation and hence is severely limited in the outlets for them. Another organization that carries on an extensive fact-finding program is the Anti-Defamation League of B'nai B'rith. But the extent and the effectiveness of the use of its findings are also limited by the hard truth that many of the people most concerned with the desegregation crisis do not want to be bothered with new facts.

How much influence these organizations can exert on functionaries is very questionable. There is no evidence that they can muster enough strength to constitute political pressure groups, or even to promise significant support to the functionary who is already persuaded of the validity of their goals. On the other hand, none of them utilizes legal pressure in the way the NAACP does. The only means of influencing functionaries that remains available for them is persuasion. The effectiveness of this means is difficult to measure. According to Peters, the American Friends Service Committee and some of the state human relations councils have been able to "play a part" in bringing about peaceful school desegregation in some communities.[21] It remains to be demonstrated, however, that they have played a decisive part in the formulation by functionaries of the decision to desegregate.

## TYPES OF COMMUNICATION

The communications function is one that many of these organizations emphasize as important. This is a time when any sort of interracial gathering is likely to evoke suspicion and even reprisals, and when communication between the races is said to have "broken down." Unquestionably the meetings, workshops and conferences which they sponsor do serve to maintain a type of communication. But it is communication between people who are already agreed on the fundamental issue but who are not, except in the case of some of the Negroes, the principal actors in the conflict.

In the meantime another type of communication between whites and Negroes still goes on—but it is an indirect type. It takes place in the context of a fundamental conflict of values, with neither side being willing to admit that the other is right. The media through which the opposing sides speak to each other are legal briefs, petitions, statements to the press, picket lines, and demonstrations. The struggle has the characteristics of a cold war, with each side demanding unconditional surrender as the price of peace. On the one hand, segregationists have rejected even "token integration" and have opposed plans for the most gradual type of integration. On the other, Negro leaders have attacked plans which called explicitly for token integration or gradual integration. Litigation, as a medium of communication and "bargaining," is costly and slow. It has often been accompanied by acrimonious debate which has served to heighten racial tensions. It has resulted inevitably in defeat for one of the litigants, with accompanying feelings of frustration, loss of face, and loss of freedom of action. In some instances the response of white people to what they have perceived as "judicial force" has been resort to other kinds of force. There have certainly been many instances in which the question might well have been asked, "What was the use of going to court in the first place?" But by and large the defenders of segregation have indicated that the most peaceful way they will deal with requests or demands for desegregation is through litigation. The events of Oxford and Birmingham have shown that when litigation fails they will resort to force.

## THE NEW NEGRO

In 1860 American society, particularly southern society, was agrarian; the Negro was a virtually helpless ward, not even of the government, but of the slaveholder or the abolitionist. A century later our society has moved far along the scale of industrialization, urbanization and impersonalization. The Negro, far from being helpless, speaks from a position of power. He has become more like the white man, yet has drawn farther away from, not closer to, the white man. A "New Negro" has emerged but, in the words of Joseph Himes,

> The newness seems . . . to inhere in the refusal to conceal, repress or compromise the spirit of militancy and resistance that has characterized some Negroes in all stations throughout our national history. . . . On the ebb and flow of racial change, the spirit of compromise and accommodation is being curtailed and the orientation towards militancy is being accentuated and glorified.[22]

The experience of Little Rock, Montgomery, New Orleans, and Birmingham dramatized the explosive potentialities of intergroup conflict in terms not only of the disruption of the educational system but also of economic loss to the business community and unfavorable publicity for the city and state. These explosive potentialities have not, of course, concerned the radical segregationist. Whether as a result of a conscious choice between values or an unrealistic assessment of the cost of resistance, he has been willing to stake all in defense of this system of segregation. Nor have the most militant Negro leaders been greatly concerned about the disruptive effects of racial conflict since their faith in the ultimate victory of their cause, their "all to gain, nothing to lose" attitude, makes community crises mere stepping stones to victory. But, even as far back as 1954, "moderates" of many varieties, both white and Negro, have regarded the threat of racial conflict as a crucial problem.

The threat of conflict has not, however, shattered the optimism of the moderates. Heightened racial tension and the specter of violence have instead spurred them to seek new forms of accommodation. The desire that peace, harmony, goodwill, and mutual understanding be restored and maintained has been a meeting ground for "moderate segregationists" and "moderate integrationists"—or, as they often describe themselves, "men of goodwill on both sides."

## THE UTOPIAN MODEL IN SOCIAL SCIENCE

Whether they knew it or not these sanguine moderates could find plentiful support for their optimism in the writings of behavioral scientists. By mid-century American sociologists and psychologists, although formally eschewing the role of the social engineer, had come to a position of implicit faith in the intrinsic harmony of social systems and the natural reasonableness of the individual. Not that the existence of social conflict and individual maladjustment has not been recognized. But these have been regarded as abnormal, transient and theoretically corrigible states. "Adjustment," including good mental health and the absence of prejudice, has been regarded as not only an attainable but also as a normal condition for the individual. On the sociological level, the prevalence of the equilibrium model of society has led some sociologists to challenge the whole emphasis on equilibrium, homeostasis, and consensus with such articles as "Out of Utopia" [23] and, "Where Is the Modern Sociology of Conflict?" [24] A sociologist discussing "social disorganization and deviant behavior" says of the central themes of much of modern sociological theory (the problem of order, the functional prerequisites of social systems, the conditions of homeostasis, of equilibrium, of boundary maintenance) :

> All of them imply a conception of a social system as a structure of interaction, which, despite the buffetings of the environment and internal stresses, manages to preserve certain characteristics. . . .

All these concepts imply, further, a particular approach to social systems—one that regards them as mechanisms for their own perpetuation.[25]

Another support for optimism could be found in the popularity of group dynamics, both as a source of hypothesis and a technique for problem solving. Although they feel that this almost cultist devotion to the theory is erroneous, Cartwright and Zander, as serious, informed social scientists utilizing the approach, say:

> According to one rather frequent usage, group dynamics refers to a sort of political ideology concerning the ways in which groups should be organized and managed. This ideology emphasizes the importance of democratic leadership, the participation of members in decisions, and the gains both to society and to individuals to be obtained through cooperative activities in groups.[26]

A similar theme of optimism and faith in social engineering of harmony has been found, and extensively criticized, in a field of sociology where conflict might be expected to be a dominant theme —"industrial sociology." Harold L. Sheppard summed up this theme in the statement:

> The common argument in this context, that industrial peace depends upon the exercise of "social skills"—of tact and forbearance— rests on the assumption that a fundamental identity of interests exists between the parties involved in industrial relations, and that this identity is increasingly interrupted by regrettable misunderstanding or breakdowns in communication.[27]

It is not surprising that this utopian theme has also pervaded much of the field of race relations. Had it not been established that all men were indeed "brothers under the skin" and that race prejudice was simply another attitude which was learned and could be unlearned? Had not Sumner's cautions against attempting to contravene the moves been replaced by faith in the power of a firm, unequivocal stand by leaders to bring about change in spite of adverse public opinion? Most important, had not Myrdal provided a cogent argument for the proposition that the race problem arose not from a conflict between whites and Negroes but from a conflict within the hearts and minds of white people?

Ten years after the publication of Myrdal's analysis, Coleman found that one of the three constants which "one or more" sociologists used in their prediction about desegregation was "the American creed—that the ideal of equality ought to control the lives of men." [28] Myrdal's assumption as to the reality and force of both the American creed and the American dilemma went almost unchallenged, except in the polemics of a few Marxist writers, until the 1960's.

As Medalia has pointed out, a corollary of Myrdal's assumption concerning the American dilemma was his assumption that the dynamics of the American race problem lay in a "strain towards consistency." [29] It is true that Myrdal quite accurately predicted that the "peace crisis" of the postwar period would be accompanied by increased tensions and violent reactions to the end of "the national compromise." But this was his prediction for the short run. His long-run prediction reflected his firm belief in the reality of the conflict of values and the potency of the impulse to resolve it:

> People want to be rational, and they want to feel that they are good and righteous. They want to have the society they live in, and their behavior in this society, explained and justified to their conscience. And now their theory is being torn to pieces; its expression is becoming recognized as a mark of ignorance.[30]

Even the emergence of the Resistance Movement in the months following the school desegregation decision of 1954 failed to disturb the faith of social scientists that, in Park's terms, assimilation would certainly follow the stage of accommodation. The declarations of segregationists that "it would never happen," the crude violence of Clinton and Little Rock, and the refined torture of boycotts were perceived as futile acts of last-ditch resistance which could, at most, simply delay the inevitable. The real question to social scientists and to lay "moderates" alike was not what the outcome of the struggle would be. It was, instead, how the inevitable end could be reached with conscionable delay, deliberate speed, and a minimum of conflict! While social scientists predicted that the process would be gradual, uneven and, at times, tumultuous, they also predicted that integration would occur and that resistance was doomed to be only a delaying action. The moderateness of the admittedly pro-segregation attitudes of the great majority of southern white people and the devotion of these people to the values of law and order, Christianity, and the public school systems were documented. The ability of public officials to neutralize the minority of radical segregationists, if only they would, was affirmed by references to instances of successful desegregation of factories, of housing projects and military units. Faith in the efficacy of the general valuations of the American creed was reasserted in numerous ways by both social scientists and by laymen who may never have read Myrdal's words.

*A Manual of Intergroup Relations,* by Dean and Rosen, suggested to professionals in the field of intergroup relations techniques for involving "persons in the power structure who are sympathetic to fair play policies" in "city-wide policy committees" which might work toward the improvement of intergroup relations.[31] It is not clear to what extent the authors felt that their suggestions might be feasible as guides to action in southern communities, but the volume was addressed to a nation-wide audience. It is fairly typical of the optimistic, "social engineering" approach which many social scientists and some laymen felt could be brought into play once the futility and destructiveness of resistance were recognized by the "gatekeepers" of states and communities.

## THE CONFLICT MODEL

But there is another theme in the social sciences with a history as long as that of the themes of equilibrium and consensus. This is the concept of conflict. In the early days of sociology, particularly in Europe, this was a dominant theme. The theories of two European sociologists, Ludwig Gumplowicz and Gustav Ratzenhofer, influenced two of the founders of American sociology, Lester F. Ward and Albion W. Small, who viewed conflict as a primary pattern of human interaction. Their theories were optimistic in the sense that both felt that conflict led to integration on higher levels. But they viewed conflict as a central social process which was functional, not merely dysfunctional, normal not pathological. Robert E. Park, E. A. Ross, and Charles H. Cooley all saw conflict as a "fundamental and constructive part of social organization." Lewis Coser says of the first generation of American sociologists,

> Conflict was seen as inherent in the social structure, and those particular types of conflict which were evaluated negatively could be eliminated, they felt, only through structural change.[32]

Of the modern generation he says, however,

> They center attention predominantly upon problems of adjustment rather than upon conflict; upon social statics rather than upon dynamics. . . . Where the older generation discussed the need for structural change, the new generation deals with adjustment of individuals to given structures. In the dominant trend of contemporary American sociology, the psychological subsumes the structural and hence individual malfunctioning subsumes social conflict.[33]

Some modern sociologists, like Coser, have recently been engaged in a rediscovery and revival of the conflict model. Coser, re-examining the propositions advanced by the German sociologist, Georg Simmel, has contributed to this revival in his book entitled *The Functions of Social Conflict*. Irving L. Horowitz, in an article criticizing overreliance on "consensus theory," argues,

> If we start from the position of real societies it is evident that conflict situations are intrinsic and organic to social structure. Considered in this manner, the group, the community, or the nation is the particularized area of social activity in which conflicts arise and are resolved.[34]

A sociologist who has regarded the conflict which arose following the desegregation decision of 1954-1955 as functional is Ernst Borinski. Perhaps he sees conflict as central, not peripheral, to the impending changes in southern society because he writes from Mississippi, where the prospects of a peaceful adjustment seemed dimmest. Borinski speaks of "the legal conflict-construct" created by the 1954 and 1955 decisions of the United States Supreme Court.[35] As he expresses it,

> Dominant and subgroups are fighting for their respective aspirations on legal grounds. Legislation and litigation are the stimulus-response reactions through which contending parties seek realization of their respective social objectives.[36]

But of greater significance is his observation,

> The 1955 decision invites further litigation so that the common ideas of the communities involved may participate in shaping law appropriate for any specific integration situation.[37]

Hence, the very nature of the 1954 and 1955 decisions of the Supreme Court invited not voluntary cooperation between white and Negro leaders but the exercise of power by the Negro minority through the threat of the invocation of federal sanctions.

## DIRECT ACTION

But in a very short time court action lost its preeminence as the method for applying the power of the Negro minority. Through experience in bus boycotts, selective buying campaigns, and nonviolent resistance, Negroes discovered other sanctions which they might apply. A study by Jacqueline J. Clark of members of Negro protest organizations in three Alabama cities discloses the faith placed by Negroes in techniques which emphasize such manifestations of the power of the Negro minority.[38] The author found that her sample showed the greatest preference for nonviolent techniques, almost 84 percent selecting these as appropriate means to achieve civil rights ends. Next was ranked the technique of holding mass meetings (55 percent), next, public relations (43 percent), and then boycotting (40 percent). Only 27 percent preferred interracial pressure as an appropriate technique, indicating the relatively low degree of confidence in unified biracial efforts. She concludes from her analysis of techniques actually used in these cities,

> The most significant of these measures both in terms of the organizational policies and programs and the uses made of them in Alabama, are (1) mass meetings; (2) nonviolent techniques, especially boycotting, or rather what Negroes refer to as "protest" inasmuch as boycotting is illegal in Alabama; and (3) legal-judiciary measures, including voting.[39]

Still, federal court action remains an important weapon in the minority's arsenal of power. In spite of the high ranking which nonviolent techniques received in this study, Clark observes that these measures seem to be most effective only under certain circumstances when resistance is low. She observes:

> When more than token resistance is offered, the principal means through which Negroes gain increasing civil rights seemed to be through gaining a significant voting power and winning victories

in the federal courts or through the intervention of the federal government in enforcing already existing legislation and investigating violations of civil rights.[40]

## VOTING AS A WEAPON

During 1962, two years after the beginning of the "revolt" symbolized by the "sit-ins" and "freedom rides," use of the ballot seemed to be gaining ground as a technique of power. Leaders of the NAACP, at their annual convention, placed a new emphasis on voting as compared with either court action or nonviolent resistance. An observer at the convention evaluated the significance of this development in these words:

> Why the new emphasis on voter registration? One hears three sorts of explanations suggested.
> 1. Direct action, even when coupled with resort to the courts, just hasn't done the job. Moreover, some kinds of segregation do not seem susceptible to direct-action techniques, particularly discrimination in employment and (to a lesser extent) in housing.
> 2. Voter registration has shown its effectiveness in assisting direct action.
> 3. The Kennedy Administration and private foundations have encouraged voter registration rather than civil disobedience.[41]

If Negroes do attempt to mass their power at the polls the result could be, of course, an increase in group cohesion and the growth of another type of antagonistic interaction with the white community. While this political conflict would be nonviolent, it still would emphasize the conflicting interests and the separate identities of the two groups.

## THE IMPORTANCE OF MINORITY POWER: A CASE STUDY

What is of most significance in this context, of course, is the indication that the strategic use of power by Negroes themselves is most effective in producing change, not the cooperative efforts of white and Negro leaders who, through communication, have discovered a common ground for action. Further support for this proposition is found in the detailed historical account of the interaction between Negro and white leaders in a southern community in a study by M. Elaine Burgess, *Negro Leadership in a Southern City*.[42] Her study is of particular interest here because, during the period covered, a commission on race relations was appointed by the mayor in "Crescent City." This committee emerged at a time when Negroes in the community were actively seeking the assignment of Negro children to white schools, and a court suit seemed imminent. In Burgess' words,

> A few individuals in both the white and Negro sub-communities, alarmed by the lack of communication on school desegregation, felt that contact and exchange should be encouraged.[43]

The white leaders who first proposed a commission are described by the author as "secondary power leaders in the white structure," and the Negro leaders advocating it are identified elsewhere in the study as "moderate Negro leaders." The proposal, once initiated, did, however, receive support from some of the more powerful, and also more conservative, leaders in the white power structure, as well as from some of the more militant Negro leaders. Some of the latter felt from the first, however, that

> The commission was a faltering and tardy effort that actually might become a stumbling block in the way of desegregation.[44]

Nevertheless, the city council was persuaded to appoint such a commission. The first task that it undertook was an attempt to bring the Negro leadership and the city school board to an agreement on school desegregation. But this initial effort met with a pointed rebuff by the board of education, which simply heard the remarks of the committee chairman and then passed on to the other business without comment. As a consequence, Burgess observes, "It was not until late in the following year that the Biracial Commission began to achieve any of its purposes. . . . In the meantime both Negroes and whites felt that the commission was all but dead." [45] At the same time, the Negro leaders of the city proceeded to bring suit to require desegregation of the city's schools.

It has been indicated above that the Biracial Committee did subsequently regain some slight measure of prestige in the community. It was, however, the use of power by a segment of the Negro

community which led to this. Students at a Negro college, led by a
very militant young Negro minister, prepared to launch a campaign
of protest against separate white and Negro "welcome college students" day sponsored by the local merchants' association. They sent
a petition charging prejudicial treatment to the association and laid
plans for a boycott and a protest parade. When threatened with the
application of these sanctions, the merchants' association turned to
the commission on race relations for help. The commission was able
to act as a mediator between student representatives and the merchants' association, facilitating an agreement which headed off the
protest campaign. This was the only accomplishment of the commission on race relations reported by Burgess, and it is evident
from the study that it played only a very minor role in race relations
in "Crescent City." The major social force operating for a change
was, instead, the continual pressure of Negro leaders for serious
readjustments in the city's power structure and the fact that, in
Burgess' words,

> The ability of minority leaders to raise Crescent City issues to
> the level of controversy has become a real source of power.[46]

## A CRITIQUE OF AMELIORATIVE STRATEGY

Forthright criticism of the extension of the optimistic, ameliorative theme of modern sociology to the field of race relations is found
in a critique of Dean and Rosen's *Manual* by James B. McKee.[47]
Although not referring to the recent writings critical of "consensus
theory" or even to Myrdal, McKee argues that the strategy suggested
in the *Manual* rests on the assumption that "the climate of opinion in
America is favorable to desirable changes in intergroup relations,"
or, in other words, on the growing efficacy of the American Creed.
From this premise stems the additional assumption that the significant people of influence in the white power structure can be induced
to become involved in a cooperative effort to improve intergroup
relations because of their increasing acceptance of equality and fair
play as a goal. Hence the strategy depends for its success upon the
involvement of these key leaders in a cooperative effort to improve
intergroup relations, not upon the exercise of power (with the con-
comitant risk of conflict) by pressure groups outside the power

structure. But, as McKee points out, Dean and Rosen themselves assume that the key leaders in a community are most likely to be drawn from the upper economic and social levels and to be ideologically conservative. On the other hand, those influentials who are willing to be identified in an effort to improve intergroup relations are likely to be in the lower levels of the power structure. The gist of McKee's criticisms of the approach suggested in *A Manual of Intergroup Relations* is that it contains a general conservative bias by virtue of its "basic ideological orientation; to operate within and not outside of, independent of, or as a challenge to the existing power structure." [48]

Confirmation of McKee's argument that the really powerful leaders in the white power structure constitute a conservatizing force is found in a study of Negro leadership in New Orleans. Daniel C. Thompson, in *The Negro Leadership Class,* analyzes not only types of Negro leaders but also their interaction with various types of white leaders.[49] He concludes,

> . . . Whites who occupy top power positions in New Orleans are pledged, or assumed to be pledged, to the preservation of a biracial social system that, according to its inherent nature, relegates all Negroes to an inferior social status. This means that Negroes who seek to achieve racial equality are automatically resisted by white men of power.[50]

## OPTIMISTIC AND PESSIMISTIC THEMES IN PUBLIC OPINION

The contrasting themes of consensus and conflict expressed in the writings of social scientists have their counterparts in expressions of optimism and pessimism about the future of race relations by laymen. Until recently the pessimistic notion that the integration of Negroes as full participants in American society could not be achieved without a major social conflict was confined largely to the so-called "die-hard" segregationists. For a man of such proven sensitivity to the Negro's plight as William Faulkner to predict, as he did in 1956, that the desegregation controversy might lead to racial warfare was exceptional and shocking to many moderates.

On the other hand, both "integrationists" and "moderate segregationists" generally expressed what was essentially an optimistic theme. They differed from each other as to how long it would take for "the problem" to be worked out, the relative importance of private acceptance and public compliance, and the means by which either could be brought about. But both types of white Americans, as well as many Negro Americans, clung to their optimism that the problem would be worked out within the framework of orderly, democratic processes because of the fundamental good will, sense of fair play and justice, and respect for law of the vast majority of Americans. Conflict would arise, but it would develop primarily because of the recalcitrance of the "lunatic fringe" of segregationists, the impatience of radical integrationists, and the slowness to act of the great mass of "middle-of-the-roaders."

## PROPOSALS FOR BIRACIAL COMMITTEES

One of the techniques most often suggested for bringing about this adjustment, this restoration of equilibrium, has been "breaking down the barriers to communication between the races." The implication is clear that this would, supposedly, restore consensus, prevent conflict, and make possible a cooperative effort by white and Negro leaders to work out the difficult problems of social engineering involved in the transition to an integrated society. A specific device suggested as a way of establishing communication was the interracial or biracial committee. As early as 1954 the Attorney General of Florida suggested to the Supreme Court of the United States that lower federal courts should consider as evidences of good faith on the part of school authorities seeking to comply with the Brown decision,

> Efforts previously made and in progress to promote citizens' educational committees and interracial committees for the purpose of improving racial relations in the community, and avoiding racial antagonism in the schools.[51]

Soon after the 1954 decision, the Southern Regional Council launched a drive to encourage the formation of biracial human relations councils throughout the South. At the same time, through its consultant program, the Council attempted to stimulate communications between white and Negro leaders in southern communities through workshops at which biracial teams of consultants would serve as resource persons.

The strongest public manifestation of faith in the value of the biracial committee in reducing racial tensions and producing peaceful change was expressed by Governor Leroy Collins of Florida during the sit-in demonstrations of the spring of 1960. In a televised address to the people of Florida, he appealed to the great body of moderates in the citizenry to assert themselves and to take the leadership in race relations. The most important concrete step which he recommended for the implementation of his philosophy was the appointment by communities of committees of leading white and Negro citizens to study problems of race relations and mediate differences before they reached the point of open conflict. At the same time he appointed a state biracial advisory committee. Governor Collins' appeal was reported in the mass media throughout the nation, largely because it represented an unusually liberal position for a southern governor. An "experiment in interracial cooperation" had been launched with his official sanction.

During the better part of the decade which has passed since that momentous Monday in May, 1954, numerous southern communities have seen their patterns of race relations change in countless ways. New organizations have sprung up to make their contributions to the process of social change; new tactics and techniques have been developed. Some communities have been rent by violent conflict; others have shifted quietly and peacefully to "token integration"; yet others have changed hardly at all. Integration has progressed, but with speed so deliberate that it can hardly be called speed. Only the most irrepressible optimist could contend that the multifaceted problem of Negro–white relations in the United States is significantly nearer to being resolved than it was in 1954. It is time to ask, "How much is optimism justified? Is the problem of race relations even more complex and difficult than it appeared when the curtain rose on the drama of the desegregation crisis?" And, particularly, we may ask, "What part have cooperation and consensus played in the process of social change as compared with conflict and the threat of conflict?" In seeking partial answers to these questions, trends in race relations in the South and in the entire nation, as well as patterns of cooperation and conflict in selected communities, will be examined.

## NOTES

1. Ina C. Brown, *Race Relations in a Democracy* (New York: Harper & Row, Publishers, 1949), p. 55.

2. *Ibid.*, p. 45.

3. Benjamin Brawley, *A Social History of the American Negro* (New York: The Macmillan Company, 1921), p. 76.

4. Henry Hughes, *Treatise on Sociology, Theoretical and Practical* (Philadelphia, 1854); George Fitzhugh, *Sociology for the South; or the Failure of Free Society* (Richmond, 1854).

5. Dred Scott v. Sanford, 19 Howard 393 (1856).

6. The National Committee on Segregation in the Nation's Capital, *Segregation in Washington* (4901 Ellis Ave., Chicago, 1948).

7. Quoted in C. Vann Woodward, *The Strange Career of Jim Crow* (New York: Oxford University Press, Inc., 1955), pp. 49-50.

8. 163 U.S. 537 (1895).

9. James M. Dabbs, *Southern Heritage* (New York: Alfred A. Knopf, Inc., 1958), p. 54.

10. Brown *et al. v.* Board of Education of Topeka *et al.,* 347 U.S. 483 (1953).

11. Robert E. Park, *Race and Culture* (New York: The Free Press of Glencoe, Inc., 1950), p. 243.

12. *With All Deliberate Speed,* edited by Don Shoemaker (New York: Harper & Row, Publishers, 1957), p. 19.

13. Quoted in Herbert Wey and John Corey, *Action Patterns in School Desegregation* (Bloomington, Ind.: Phi Delta Kappa, Inc., 1959), p. 31.

14. *Race Relations Law Reporter* 224, 1959.

15. Herbert Blumer, "Social Science and the Desegregation Process," *The Annals of the American Academy of Political and Social Science,* Vol. 304, March, 1956, p. 142.

16. *Ibid.,* p. 142.

17. Harold Fleming, "Resistance Movements and Racial Desegregation," *The Annals,* Vol. 304, March, 1956, p. 44.

18. *Ibid.,* p. 51.

19. Southern Regional Council, *Special Report,* "Organizations and Personnel Engaged in Human Relations Activities in the South." 63 Auburn Ave., N.E., Atlanta, Georgia, May 1, 1957.

20. William Peters, *The Southern Temper* (Garden City, N.Y.: Doubleday & Company, Inc., 1959), p. 170.

21. *Ibid.,* pp. 170f.

22. Joseph Himes, "Changing Social Roles in the New South," *Southwest Social Science Quarterly* (December, 1956), pp. 240-41.

23. Ralf Dahrendorf, "Out of Utopia: Toward a Reorientation of Sociological Analysis," *American Journal of Sociology,* 64 (1958), pp. 115-27.

24. Jessie Bernard, "Where Is the Modern Sociology of Conflict?" *American Journal of Sociology,* 56 (1950), pp. 11-16.

25. Albert K. Cohen, "Social Disorganization and Deviant Behavior," in *Sociology Today,* edited by Roger K. Merton, Leonard Broom, and L. S. Cottrell, Jr. (New York: Basic Books, Inc., 1959), p. 483.

26. Dorwin Cartwright and Alvin Zander, eds. *Group Dynamics: Research and Theory* (2nd ed.) (New York: Harper & Row, Publishers, 1960), p. 5.

27. Harold L. Sheppard, "The Treatment of Unionism in 'Managerial' Sociology," *American Sociological Review*, 14 (1949), pp. 311-12.

28. A. Lee Coleman, "Social Scientists' Predictions About Desegregation," *Social Forces*, 38 (1960), pp. 258-61.

29. Nahum Medalia, "Myrdal's Assumptions on Race Relations: A Conceptual Commentary," *Social Forces*, 40 (1962), p. 225.

30. *An American Dilemma* (New York: Harper & Row, Publishers, 1944), p. 1003.

31. John Dean and Bernard Rosen, *A Manual of Intergroup Relations* (Chicago: University of Chicago Press, 1955).

32. Lewis Coser, *The Functions of Social Conflict* (New York: The Free Press of Glencoe, Inc., 1956), p. 19.

33. *Ibid.*, p. 20.

34. "Consensus, Conflict and Cooperation," *Social Forces*, 41 (1962), p. 180.

35. Ernst Borinski, "The Litigation Curve and the Litigation Filibuster in Civil Rights Cases," *Social Forces*, 37 (1958), pp. 142-47.

36. *Ibid.*, p. 142.

37. *Ibid.*, p. 144.

38. Jacqueline J. Clark, "Standard Operational Procedures in Tragic Situations," *Phylon* (4th Quarter, 1961), pp. 318-28.

39. *Ibid.*, p. 323.

40. *Ibid.*, p. 325.

41. Staughton Lynd, "Freedom Riders to the Polls," *The Nation*, 195 (July 28, 1962), p. 30.

42. Chapel Hill: University of North Carolina Press, 1960.

43. *Ibid.*, p. 126.

44. *Ibid.*, p. 129.

45. *Ibid.*, p. 132.

46. *Ibid.*, p. 193.

47. James McKee, "Community Power and Strategies in Race Relations: Some Critical Observations," *Social Problems* (Winter, 1958-59), pp. 195-203.

48. *Ibid.*, p. 200.

49. Englewood Cliffs, N.J.: Prentice-Hall, Inc., 1963.

50. *Ibid.*, p. 165.

51. *Amicus curiae* brief of the Attorney General of Florida in the case of Oliver, Brown, *et al.*, *v.* Board of Education of Topeka, Kansas, in the Supreme Court of the United States, October term, 1954, p. 62.

TWO

# An Experiment in Cooperation:
# The Community
# Biracial Committee

In order to ascertain to what extent the biracial committee had actually been adopted as a technique of communication in southern communities, early in 1962 the Institute for Social Research of the Florida State University sent questionnaires to the mayors or city managers of 389 communities in 12 southern states.[1] This included all cities with a 1960 population of 10,000 or over. Three hundred and thirty-six questionnaires were returned, giving a total response rate of 86.3 percent. It is likely that a great majority of those communities whose officials did not respond did not have a biracial committee. This survey showed that of the 336 communities, only 55, or 16.4 percent, had appointed biracial committees. Five of the communities reported that they had such committees even prior to 1954, but the fact that the spread of this device is a recent phenomenon is indicated by the fact that while only nine committees were appointed between 1954 and 1959, 39 were created in the three years 1959 through 1961. The reason given most frequently for considering the appointment of such a committee was "to improve race relations." The reason next most frequently mentioned was the occurrence or the threat of sit-ins. This was cited 13 times, or in 24 percent of the communities. This fact, plus the time during which most of the committees were appointed (a period during which the sit-ins were the most prominent manifestation of the Negro protest movement) supports the theme that the fear of public disorder stemming out of minority demonstrations is one of the most important stimuli for the creation of the biracial committee.

## A CASE STUDY: A BIRACIAL COMMITTEE IN ACTION

A survey of this type did not, of course, reveal the extent of the activity of the committees which were reported. It was found that 37, or 62 percent, of the committees had held meetings some time during the year preceding the survey and could be assumed to be still in existence. In anticipation of the superficial nature of questionnaire findings, a case study of a biracial committee appointed in 1960 had already been undertaken. This case study was carried out in conjunction with a community satisfaction survey. Dean and Rosen have suggested that one of the most important factors which might facilitate communication about problems of race relations between white and Negro leaders is the possession of facts concerning conditions and attitudes in the community which they represent. The approach used here departed from the suggestion of Dean and Rosen that a community self-survey be used to provide such facts. Instead, an independent survey, planned and directed by professional sociologists, was used to provide data which would be presented to the biracial committee at an opportune time in its career. The primary purpose of the case study was to analyze the interaction between the white and Negro leaders and between the committee and the community. The function of the community survey was to provide entrée into the deliberations of the committee and, if need be, to provide material toward which the interaction of the members could focus.

The committee chosen for this case study was located in a community in which conditions seemed optimal for the success of this technique of communication. It was one of the first cities in the state to respond to Governor Collins' appeal for the appointment of biracial committees. Although there was a suit in the federal courts challenging school segregation in the county, and a boycott in support of lunch-counter desegregation being sponsored by the local chapter of the NAACP, neither of these activities had led to overt racial conflict, arrests, or any ostensible heightening of tension in the community. The local newspaper was known throughout the state for its unusually liberal editorial policy in matters of race relations. The city had employed Negro policemen and Negro bus drivers for several years. Although segregation was the prevailing pattern, interracial workshops, conferences, and church services caused no particular comment and evoked no harassment when they were held in the community. This certainly seemed to be the type of southern community in which one would be most likely to find, in the words of Dean and Rosen, "persons in the power structure who are sympathetic to fair play policies." [2]

The 1960 population of this city was shown by the Bureau of the Census to be approximately 38,000. The Negro population constituted approximately 30 percent of the total. It was also known that a sizable proportion of the white population consisted of migrants from northern states. Like many other Florida communities of this size, the city depended primarily upon the tourist industry for its economic welfare.

In this setting, the case study of a biracial committee in action was undertaken. Since one part of the study of the process of communication was to be an analysis of the committee's reaction to the feedback of community survey data to them, the execution of the community satisfaction survey constituted the first stage of the research.

## THE COMMUNITY SURVEY

With the cognizance, but not the sponsorship, of the city commission, a community survey was inaugurated quietly. The survey was based on interviews with 502 white and 596 Negro subjects selected by a cluster sampling technique. Only permanent residents eighteen years of age or older were drawn in the samples.

The interview schedule was designed to obtain two general types of data. The first consisted of background information reflecting the socioeconomic characteristics of the subjects. It included questions on age, marital status, education, occupation, migration history, income, voting behavior, household conveniences, home ownership, car ownership, and labor-union membership. The second section consisted of questions concerning "community satisfaction." One series of questions asked how the subject felt about specific types of services or opportunities offered by the community—employment, schools, public health services, recreational facilities, police services, and housing. The interview was concluded with several general questions concerning what the subject liked best about the city and what he thought were the greatest needs of the community.

The survey results reflected the generally lower educational level and socioeconomic status of the Negroes. Their concentration in the lower educational levels was documented, as shown in Table 1.

TABLE 1

Percent Distribution of Education, by Race and Sex

| Education | WHITE | | NEGRO | |
|---|---|---|---|---|
| | Male | Female | Male | Female |
| None or some grade school | 8.7 | 3.8 | 33.3 | 23.6 |
| 8th grade—some high school | 29.3 | 31.1 | 38.4 | 45.2 |
| 12th grade—some college | 42.4 | 56.6 | 25.8 | 27.8 |
| College or beyond | 19.6 | 8.5 | 2.5 | 3.4 |
| Total percent | 100.0 | 100.0 | 100.0 | 100.0 |
| Total number | 184 | 318 | 240 | 356 |

Slightly over one third of both male and female white subjects had not completed high school. But the problem of undereducation was even more acute among Negroes. Over two thirds of them, whether male or female, did not have a complete high school education. Of the Negro men, a third had not even finished the eighth grade, and almost one fourth of the Negro women had not finished the eighth grade.

The underrepresentation of Negroes in white-collar jobs is revealed in Table 2. Three things stand out in this table. One is the fact that a much higher proportion of white women than of Negro women were housewives. This may reflect the difference in marital status of white and Negro women, with a much higher proportion of the white women being married. The question might also be raised, however, as to whether the higher proportion of Negro women who work may contribute to greater family disorganization among Negroes. The second thing to be noted is the very low representation of Negroes in occupations classified as "manager, proprietor, clerical and sales." Clerical jobs represented the most important source of occupation for white females who were employed, but less than one half of one percent of Negro women reported this type of employment. For Negro women who worked, the most important type of occupation was in service and household work, which includes domestic service and work as maids or cleaning women in motels, hotels, or restaurants. The Negro men found their greatest opportunity for employment in service work or as unskilled laborers.

TABLE 2

Percent Distribution of Occupation, by Race and Sex

| | WHITE | | NEGRO | |
| Occupation | Male | Female | Male | Female |
| --- | --- | --- | --- | --- |
| Professional | 15.2 | 5.7 | 5.0 | 2.2 |
| Managerial, prop. | 15.8 | 4.4 | 2.5 | .8 |
| Clerical | 5.4 | 9.7 | .4 | .3 |
| Sales | 7.6 | 4.4 | .4 | — |
| Crafts, foreman | 10.3 | .3 | 10.4 | — |
| Operatives | 7.1 | 2.2 | 15.0 | 4.8 |
| Service, household | 10.3 | 5.4 | 27.1 | 49.4 |
| Laborers | 4.9 | — | 26.3 | — |
| Housewife | — | 58.2 | — | 35.2 |
| Other* | 23.4 | 9.7 | 12.9 | 7.3 |
| Total percent | 100.0 | 100.0 | 100.0 | 100.0 |
| Total number | 184 | 318 | 240 | 356 |

* "Other" includes unemployed, retired, disabled, student, no response.

Negroes were found to constitute a native population to a much greater extent than the whites (Table 3). Moreover, the Negroes who were migrants had, prior to movement to this city, lived in smaller communities to a much greater extent than had white migrants. Table 3 shows that almost one half of the Negroes were born in Florida, but only about 15 percent of the whites were. When we add to this the percentage who were born in other southeastern states, we see that almost all of the Negroes are natives of the South, but slightly less than half of the whites are native southerners.

TABLE 3

Distribution of Place of Birth by Race

| Place of Birth | WHITE | | NEGRO | |
|---|---|---|---|---|
| | Number | Percent | Number | Percent |
| Florida City | 22 | 4.4 | 92 | 15.4 |
| Other Florida | 53 | 10.5 | 196 | 32.9 |
| Other South | 170 | 33.9 | 294 | 49.3 |
| Other United States | 222 | 44.2 | 10 | 1.7 |
| Foreign countries | 35 | 7.0 | 3 | .5 |
| No response | — | — | 1 | .2 |
| Totals | 502 | 100.0 | 596 | 100.0 |

When we consider length of residence (Table 4), we see that 15.4 percent of the Negroes were born in this city while only 4.4 percent of the whites are natives. On the other hand, 56.2 percent of the white sample had lived there only ten years, or less, at the time of the interview, while only 33.4 percent of the Negroes were such relative newcomers.

TABLE 4

Distribution of Length of Residence in Florida City by Race

| Year Moved to City | WHITE | | NEGRO | |
|---|---|---|---|---|
| | Number | Percent | Number | Percent |
| 1900-1909 | 4 | .8 | 9 | 1.5 |
| 1910-1919 | 6 | 1.2 | 18 | 3.0 |
| 1920-1929 | 36 | 7.2 | 58 | 9.8 |
| 1930-1939 | 39 | 7.8 | 67 | 11.3 |
| 1940-1949 | 109 | 21.7 | 151 | 25.3 |
| 1950-1959 | 259 | 51.6 | 190 | 31.9 |
| 1960 | 23 | 4.6 | 9 | 1.5 |
| No response | 4 | .8 | 2 | .3 |
| Not applicable* | 22 | 4.4 | 92 | 15.4 |
| Totals | 502 | 100.0 | 596 | 100.0 |

* Born in City.

Prior to movement to this city, 44.4 percent of the Negroes lived in communities of less than 10,000 population (Table 5). In

TABLE 5

Percent Distribution of Size of Community Lived in
Prior to Moving to Florida City, by Race

| Size of Community | WHITE | NEGRO |
|---|---|---|
| Under 2500 | 13.5 | 19.6 |
| 2500-10,000 | 16.1 | 24.8 |
| 10,000-25,000 | 10.6 | 12.1 |
| 25,000-50,000* | 13.1* | 24.7* |
| Over 50,000 | 45.3 | 18.3 |
| No response | — | .3 |
| Data not available | 1.4 | .2 |
| Total percent | 100.0 | 100.0 |
| Total number | 502 | 596 |

* Of the number of respondents living in a community of this size, 4.4 percent white and 15.4 percent Negro were born in the city.

contrast, 45.2 percent of the whites had lived in communities of over 50,000 population. It may be that this difference in background has an important effect upon the attitudes of the two groups toward this city as a place to live, since many of them have different standards by which to judge it.

## LIVING CONDITIONS

It is not easy to portray through mere statistics how large numbers of people live. An attempt was made to do so, however, by two measures. One was monthly income. The second was a composite picture of what necessities and conveniences the subjects had been able to purchase with this income. Table 6 shows the distribution of income by race and sex. Without regard to race, women earned less than men. It is equally obvious that the income level of the average Negro was much lower than that of the average white worker.

## TABLE 6

### Percent Distribution of Income, by Race and Sex

| Monthly Salary | WHITE | | NEGRO | |
|---|---|---|---|---|
| | Male | Female | Male | Female |
| Under $200 | 14.1 | 26.8 | 41.3 | 68.0 |
| $200-299 | 16.4 | 7.9 | 40.4 | 3.9 |
| $300-399 | 19.0 | 5.4 | 9.2 | .8 |
| $400-499 | 19.0 | 4.7 | 2.5 | 1.2 |
| $500-599 | 7.1 | .9 | 1.3 | .3 |
| $600-699 | 4.9 | .6 | — | — |
| $700 and over | 9.8 | .3 | — | — |
| No response | 5.4 | 4.7 | 2.1 | 2.2 |
| None* | 4.3 | 48.7 | 3.3 | 23.6 |
| Total percent | 100.0 | 100.0 | 100.1 | 100.0 |
| Total number | 184 | 318 | 240 | 356 |

* Includes unemployed, housewives, etc.

Table 7 is a summary table showing the percentage of whites and Negroes owning various necessities or conveniences. First, it is seen that the percentage of home ownership was twice as great among whites as among Negroes. Also, almost twice as many whites as Negroes owned automobiles. There was a great disparity in the

## TABLE 7

### Percent Distribution of Selected Measures of Level of Living, by Race

| Percent who: | WHITE | NEGRO |
|---|---|---|
| Own homes | 70.7 | 33.1 |
| Have hot and cold running water | 95.8 | 81.9 |
| Have electricity in home | 100.0 | 98.8 |
| Have electric or gas refrigerator | 99.8 | 96.8 |
| Have tub or shower | 100.0 | 95.3 |
| Have telephone | 86.5 | 49.2 |
| Have television | 93.0 | 83.1 |
| Have radio only | 5.8 | 12.8 |
| Own automobile | 83.5 | 46.2 |
| Use city bus once a week or more | 24.1 | 54.5 |

percentages who had telephones in their homes. While the data from which this table was prepared showed that almost all the members of both groups had running water inside their dwelling places, almost 20 percent of the Negroes did not have both hot and cold running water. On the other hand, electricity, mechanical refrigerators, and tubs or showers were almost universal conveniences in both groups. The great majority of both groups owned TV sets and most of those who did not have television had radio. Only 1.2 percent of the white sample and 4.2 percent of the Negro sample had neither radio nor television in the home. The lower percentage of car ownership among Negroes is reflected in another figure—the percentage of subjects who use the city buses regularly. Over twice as many Negroes as whites used the city buses once a week or more.

## COMMUNITY SATISFACTION

The measures of community satisfaction did not show that Negroes subjectively felt their disadvantage to the extent that the data on living conditions might suggest. They were not markedly more dissatisfied with their own jobs than were whites (Table 8), and they were decidedly more optimistic about job opportunities for young people (Table 9). This was interpreted as reflecting the Ne-

TABLE 8

Percent Distribution of Job Satisfaction, by Race and Sex

| Satisfaction | WHITE | | NEGRO | |
|---|---|---|---|---|
| | Male | Female | Male | Female |
| Very satisfied | 37.5 | 35.8 | 23.3 | 19.7 |
| Satisfied | 47.3 | 55.0 | 53.4 | 57.6 |
| Dissatisfied | 12.5 | 6.4 | 17.5 | 15.7 |
| Very dissatisfied | 1.1 | .6 | 3.3 | 1.4 |
| No response | 1.6 | 1.6 | 2.1 | 4.5 |
| Other* | — | .6 | .4 | 1.1 |
| Total percent | 100.0 | 100.0 | 100.0 | 100.0 |
| Total number | 184 | 318 | 240 | 356 |

* Includes housewives, unemployed, etc.

TABLE 9

Percent Distribution of Perceptions of Young People's Chances for Work, by Race and Sex

| | WHITE | | NEGRO | |
|---|---|---|---|---|
| Chances | Male | Female | Male | Female |
| Very favorable | 1.1 | .3 | 1.2 | 2.2 |
| Favorable | 16.8 | 20.8 | 33.3 | 38.2 |
| Unfavorable | 60.9 | 60.4 | 49.2 | 45.5 |
| Very unfavorable | 17.9 | 15.7 | 13.8 | 10.7 |
| Don't know, no response | 3.3 | 2.8 | 2.5 | 3.4 |
| Total percent | 100.0 | 100.0 | 100.0 | 100.0 |
| Total number | 184 | 318 | 240 | 356 |

groes' perception of the tourist industry as a source of job opportunities for them, even if the jobs were unskilled.

On most other measures of satisfaction, Negroes expressed a greater degree of dissatisfaction than did whites (Tables 10, 11, 12, 13, 14). Only in the area of housing, however, did more than half of the Negroes show dissatisfaction.

TABLE 10

Percent Distribution of Satisfaction with Educational Facilities, by Race and Sex

| | WHITE | | NEGRO | |
|---|---|---|---|---|
| Satisfaction | Male | Female | Male | Female |
| Very satisfied | 12.0 | 14.8 | 6.2 | 4.8 |
| Satisfied | 50.0 | 47.1 | 48.8 | 56.7 |
| Dissatisfied | 20.6 | 23.3 | 35.4 | 30.9 |
| Very dissatisfied | 3.8 | 4.4 | 5.4 | 3.4 |
| Don't know, no response | 13.6 | 10.4 | 4.2 | 4.2 |
| Total percent | 100.0 | 100.0 | 100.0 | 100.0 |
| Total number | 184 | 318 | 240 | 356 |

TABLE 11

Percent Distribution of Satisfaction with Recreational Facilities,
by Race and Sex

| Satisfaction | WHITE | | NEGRO | |
| | Male | Female | Male | Female |
|---|---|---|---|---|
| Very satisfied | 17.4 | 20.1 | 3.3 | 2.5 |
| Satisfied | 59.8 | 55.0 | 36.7 | 43.3 |
| Dissatisfied | 15.2 | 20.2 | 47.1 | 41.0 |
| Very dissatisfied | 5.4 | 2.2 | 8.8 | 8.4 |
| Don't know, no response | 2.2 | 2.5 | 4.2 | 4.8 |
| Total percent | 100.0 | 100.0 | 100.0 | 100.0 |
| Total number | 184 | 318 | 240 | 356 |

## COMMUNITY SATISFACTION SCORES: A COMPOSITE

To get an over-all picture of community satisfaction, answers to questions about various aspects of the community—job satisfaction, housing, education, recreational facilities, public health and medical facilities, and police protection and services—were combined into a composite score for each subject. This provided a series of "satisfac-

TABLE 12

Percent Distribution of Satisfaction with Public Health and
Medical Facilities, by Race and Sex

| Satisfaction | WHITE | | NEGRO | |
| | Male | Female | Male | Female |
|---|---|---|---|---|
| Very satisfied | 9.3 | 11.3 | 4.6 | 6.2 |
| Satisfied | 55.4 | 57.9 | 62.1 | 61.8 |
| Dissatisfied | 24.4 | 22.3 | 25.4 | 21.3 |
| Very dissatisfied | 7.1 | 4.7 | 2.9 | 4.2 |
| Don't know, no response | 3.8 | 3.8 | 5.0 | 6.5 |
| Total percent | 100.0 | 100.0 | 100.0 | 100.0 |
| Total number | 184 | 318 | 240 | 356 |

TABLE 13

Percent Distribution of Satisfaction with Police Protection
and Services, by Race and Sex

| Satisfaction | WHITE | | NEGRO | |
| --- | --- | --- | --- | --- |
| | Male | Female | Male | Female |
| Very satisfied | 16.3 | 13.2 | 2.1 | 2.8 |
| Satisfied | 61.4 | 64.2 | 63.8 | 62.3 |
| Dissatisfied | 18.5 | 17.3 | 25.8 | 25.3 |
| Very dissatisfied | 1.6 | 2.2 | 7.1 | 5.1 |
| Don't know, no response | 2.2 | 3.1 | 1.2 | 4.5 |
| Total percent | 100.0 | 100.0 | 100.0 | 100.0 |
| Total number | 184 | 318 | 240 | 356 |

tion scores," or "perfect score types." These ranged from "zero," indicating low over-all satisfaction, to "63," indicating high over-all satisfaction. Table 15 shows the satisfaction scores of white and Negro males and females. It is obvious that the over-all satisfaction of the white subjects with the community, regardless of sex, was higher than that of the Negroes. But the distribution of the scores of the Negroes is peculiar. For both males and females, there is a concentration of very low scores, indicating great dissatisfaction, and

TABLE 14

Percent Distribution of Satisfaction with Housing Opportunities,
by Race and Sex

| Satisfaction | WHITE | | NEGRO | |
| --- | --- | --- | --- | --- |
| | Male | Female | Male | Female |
| Very satisfied | 26.6 | 21.4 | 2.9 | 3.4 |
| Satisfied | 53.3 | 58.8 | 35.4 | 41.0 |
| Dissatisfied | 18.5 | 15.1 | 47.5 | 44.1 |
| Very dissatisfied | 1.1 | 2.8 | 12.9 | 8.7 |
| Don't know, no response | .5 | 1.9 | 1.3 | 2.8 |
| Total percent | 100.0 | 100.0 | 100.0 | 100.0 |
| Total number | 184 | 318 | 240 | 356 |

TABLE 15

Percent Distribution of Satisfaction Scores, by Race and Sex

| Satisfaction Score | WHITE | | NEGRO | |
|---|---|---|---|---|
| | Male | Female | Male | Female |
| 0 (Low) | 10.1 | 7.4 | 22.2 | 21.4 |
| 1 | 5.4 | 5.4 | 8.2 | 6.0 |
| 3 | 1.4 | 4.2 | 7.7 | 7.8 |
| 7 | — | 1.9 | 15.5 | 11.0 |
| 15 | 5.4 | 7.4 | 10.6 | 8.9 |
| 31 | 60.1 | 52.5 | 15.5 | 16.4 |
| 63 (High) | 17.6 | 21.2 | 20.3 | 28.5 |
| Total percent | 100.0 | 100.0 | 100.0 | 100.0 |
| Total number | 148 | 259 | 207 | 281 |

very high scores, indicating a high degree of satisfaction. Table 16, which shows the distribution of the satisfaction scores of Negro subjects by age, indicates a general tendency for younger Negroes to be more dissatisfied than the older Negroes. Table 17, showing the distribution of satisfaction scores of Negroes by education, suggests that it is Negroes who have completed high school, but have not completed college, who are most likely to have low satisfaction scores. This again seems to reflect the gap in the employment picture

TABLE 16

Percent Distribution of Satisfaction Scores of Negroes, by Age

| Satisfaction Score | 18-19 | 20-29 | 30-39 | 40-49 | 50-59 | 60-69 | 70 plus |
|---|---|---|---|---|---|---|---|
| 0 (Low) | 35.0 | 25.2 | 24.8 | 16.7 | 16.4 | 15.1 | 20.0 |
| 1 | 5.0 | 8.1 | 7.7 | 8.8 | 4.5 | 3.0 | — |
| 3 | 5.0 | 11.4 | 8.5 | 7.8 | 4.5 | — | 6.7 |
| 7 | 15.0 | 12.2 | 13.9 | 10.8 | 19.5 | 6.1 | 13.3 |
| 15 | 10.0 | 7.3 | 5.4 | 15.8 | 8.9 | 21.2 | — |
| 31 | 5.0 | 16.3 | 16.4 | 17.6 | 14.9 | 15.2 | 20.0 |
| 63 (High) | 25.0 | 19.5 | 23.3 | 22.5 | 31.3 | 39.4 | 40.0 |
| Total percent | 100.0 | 100.0 | 100.0 | 100.0 | 100.0 | 100.0 | 100.0 |
| Total number | 20 | 123 | 129 | 102 | 67 | 33 | 15 |

for Negroes between professional work, such as teaching, and semi-skilled or unskilled labor, which does not require a great deal of education.

Although the existence of a greater residue of dissatisfaction among Negroes than among whites was indicated, answers to open-ended questions suggested that the reasons expressed for this dissatisfaction were quite similar to those expressed by "dissatisfied"

TABLE 17

Percent Distribution of Satisfaction Scores of Negroes, by Education

| Satisfaction Score: | None; some grade | Completed 8th grade; some high school | Completed high school | Some college | Completed college or beyond |
|---|---|---|---|---|---|
| 0 (Low) | 16.9 | 16.5 | 34.0 | 33.3 | 25.0 |
| 1 | 4.0 | 9.0 | 6.8 | 6.1 | 6.4 |
| 3 | 4.8 | 8.0 | 8.8 | 15.2 | 6.3 |
| 7 | 10.5 | 17.5 | 8.7 | 6.1 | 12.5 |
| 15 | 19.4 | 8.0 | 3.9 | 6.1 | — |
| 31 | 20.2 | 15.1 | 12.6 | 21.1 | 6.4 |
| 63 (High) | 24.2 | 25.9 | 25.2 | 12.1 | 43.8 |
| Total percent | 100.0 | 100.0 | 100.0 | 100.0 | 100.0 |
| Total number | 124 | 212 | 103 | 33 | 16 |

whites. The ranking of "needs of the community" was quite similar for the two groups, with more industry, better roads and sidewalks, better schools, better sanitation and drainage, and more and better recreational facilities ranking highest. The desegregation of schools, recreational facilities, and other public facilities ranked lowest in the Negroes' hierarchy of expressed needs (Table 18).

Here, then, was a sketch of how Negroes lived in Florida City and how they felt about their living conditions. In some respects they proved to be quite similar to their white fellow-citizens, but there were also marked dissimilarities. Although Negroes in this community were undoubtedly "better off" than Negroes in many other communities, their position relative to white people was the same.

They were socially and culturally inferior. Their problems were those that faced Negroes all over the nation—undereducation, low income,

TABLE 18

Rank Order of Weighted Percents: Greatest Needs of the Community

| Rank | WHITE | NEGRO |
|------|-------|-------|
| 1 | More industry, business, better working conditions, wages | More industry, business, better working conditions, wages |
| 2 | Better roads, sidewalks | More, better schools and school system |
| 3 | More, better schools and school system | Better roads, sidewalks |
| 4 | Better city government | Better housing, lower taxes |
| 5 | Sanitation, drainage | More, better recreational, cultural facilities |
| 6 | More, better recreational, cultural facilities | Sanitation, drainage |
| 7 | More advertising, tourist attractions, etc. | Better city government |
|  |  | Better Negro facilities |
| 8 | General; none, "Can't think of any" |  |
| 9 | Better doctors and medical facilities | Equality in employment |
| 10 | Better housing, lower taxes | General; none, "Can't think of any." |
| 11 |  | Better doctors, cheaper medical, public welfare facilities |
| 12 |  | Better racial understanding |
| 13 |  | Equality—general |
| 14 |  | General integration |
| 15 |  | Integration of beach |
| 16 |  | Unrestricted use of public facilities |
| 17 |  | Integration of schools |
| 18 |  | Integration of theaters |

occupational inferiority, inadequate housing, and segregation. Although the level of racial tension was low in Florida City, the conditions that underlie the problem of Negro–white relations everywhere in the United States were there.

## THE FEEDBACK OF RESEARCH FINDINGS
## TO THE COMMUNITY

During the period of almost a year since the study began, the official Biracial Committee had become active. It had met periodically and at one of its meetings had advised the City Commission to open the municipal golf course to Negro players. This recommendation had been accepted by the Commission and the new policy put into effect. Hence, the Committee, existing only on paper at the time the survey was being conducted, was now a functioning organization. It was decided to present the results of the survey to this body as a means of inaugurating the feedback phase.

This Committee had been created in June, 1960, by resolution of the City Commission. The resolution stated that the purpose of the Committee would be "advising the City Commission in respect of any and all racial problems arising in the city," and that it should be composed of twelve white persons and twelve Negro persons to be appointed by the City Commission. The "charter" also provided that a quorum should consist of eight white members and eight colored members, with no action being effective unless such a quorum was present. The chairman of the Committee, one of .the white members, was elected at the first meeting. It was to him that the Mayor referred the research team for the initial contact with the Committee.

It was now possible to proceed with the second phase of the study, which included the structure and function of the Biracial Committee and the reactions of its members to the survey findings. Since the Committee was just entering the second year of its existence at the time this report was written, the study constitutes an analysis of its first year. The analysis is based on two meetings with the Committee in regular sessions and individual interviews with twenty of its twenty-four members after the second meeting, plus follow-up interviews with key members, white and Negro, during the subsequent year. As it turned out, this constituted a life history of the committee during its entire career.

## THE ACCOMPLISHMENTS OF A BIRACIAL COMMITTEE

Although the Biracial Committee was appointed partly in response to a plea of the Governor for the appointment of such committees in all cities in the state, it was not the first in this city. In 1955 a similar committee had been created on the initiative of the incumbent City Commission. There was only one major difference in the resolutions creating the two committees: a provision in the charter of the second one that if any member should miss two consecutive meetings without being excused by the chairman, he should be replaced. Members who had served on both committees felt that this was an important addition to the resolution. The first Committee had remained in active existence for approximately two years, and according to accounts of some of the members, attendance at the meetings had become very poor, and the meetings very irregular. Eventually the chairman, who had been appointed in the resolution creating the Committee, resigned because of his appointment to a judicial position. No new chairman was appointed and the Committee ceased to meet.

Possibly it was the history of having a Biracial Committee in the community that caused the City Commission to be one of the first in the state to act upon the Governor's suggestion that such committees be created. Less than a week after the Governor's plea over a state-wide television broadcast the Mayor publicly announced the intention of the City Commission to re-establish such a committee in the community. Not until three months later, however, did the City Commission pass a resolution actually creating it, and it was three months after that before the Committee actually held its first meeting.

## APPOINTMENT OF THE COMMITTEE

During the three months before passage of the resolution, the Mayor received a number of letters from groups in the community actively interested in the improvement of race relations. One was from a Negro men's group suggesting Negroes they felt would be desirable members of the group. The other letters were from an interracial group, urging that each lay group in the community having an interracial membership should have a representative on the Biracial Committee. Eight organizations were listed, and it was suggested that each be allowed to choose its own representative. The Mayor did request and receive from this organization a list of two persons, one of each race, from each of the eight organizations suggested, but only one of these persons was appointed.

This suggestion, although not acted upon, carries some interesting implications. One is whether the actual appointment of eight of the twenty-four members from interracial organizations might have created a homogeneous bloc on the Committee. Even if the members of this group were not individually committed to a policy of desegregation, the interracial character of the organizations they represented might well have given this impression. This could have created a negative reaction to the entire Committee among many citizens of the community, as well as causing an enduring schism within the Committee itself. This method of selecting members might also have suggested that the Committee constituted a congress of organizational representatives rather than a nonpartisan board of individual citizens. In this case avowedly pro-segregation groups might well have demanded equal representation, thereby increasing the danger of a permanent and destructive schism in the Committee.

It is doubtful, however, that these were the considerations which caused the City Commission to disregard the suggestions of the interracial organization. A more likely consideration was the desire of the Commissioners to appoint members, particularly white members, who were personally known to them through business and civic activities and who were free from any taint of "radicalism." In pursuing this policy the Commissioners found some difficulty in getting well-known business and civic leaders to agree to serve on the Committee. Twelve members, seven white and five Negro, were members of the old board who were simply reappointed. Interestingly, most of these persons were not asked whether they would be willing to serve; they learned of their reappointment when they read it in the paper. The twelve new members were informed by a City Commisisoner before their appointments were announced.

While the suggestions of the interracial organization were almost totally disregarded, the recommendations of the Negro men's group apparently received more consideration. Six of the twelve Negroes appointed to the new Committee were members of this organization, four of them having been specifically suggested by it.

The only public criticism of the new Committee came from the interracial organization and the local newspaper, both commonly identified in the community as "liberal" in their approach to race relations. The criticism centered around two points: the fact that no women were appointed to the Committee, and the existence of the quorum rule. The requirement that two thirds of the members of each racial group must be present for a quorum raised the fear that a small group of white members could prevent the Committee from acting by their continued absence. The Mayor felt the criticism unjust, particularly in view of its source. He felt that the very creation of the Biracial Committee constituted something of a concession to the desires of liberal groups in the community and that their criticism reflected a lack of appreciation for his boldness in urging such a step. The quorum rule reflected, of course, the fear of white Commissioners that a devoted group of Negro members attending every meeting could outvote the white members and determine the Committee's policy.

During the first six months of the Committee's existence five white members and one Negro resigned. During the next six months the membership stabilized, and at the end of the year all the members were reappointed for a second term. These members are considered in the following analysis of the Committee.

## COMPOSITION OF THE COMMITTEE

Nine of the white members were native southerners, while three were born in the North. Eight were businessmen, three were professional men, and one was a municipal employee. The professional men included a doctor, a lawyer, and a high school principal. These members' evaluation of their own and each other's influence indicated that only two white members could be ranked in the top level of influence in the community. One was the chairman, who had many business interests in the community in addition to his own business. He had lived in the community since childhood, and his father had served as mayor of the city. The other white members, if not part of the top level of the power structure, were all close enough to it to be acquainted personally with the men they described as the top leaders of the community.

The Negroes, on the other hand, were drawn primarily from the top level of the Negro community. One Negro member stated frankly that he felt the Negro members were a more influential group with their own people than were the whites. This is not to imply, however, that the Negro leaders on the Committee constituted a homogeneous or well-knit clique who ran the Negro community. Instead, they represented a variety of types of influence. They also differed in their orientations to the Negro community and its problems.

One Negro member was high in the administration of a private Negro college located in the community, and three others were on its faculty. One member was a semi-skilled laborer, four were independent business men, and the other three were professional men: a lawyer, a minister, and a public school teacher. This last member was the only Negro whose professional employment was dependent upon the approval of a white employer.

In view of the fact that these Negroes had been appointed by an all-white City Commission, it was surprising to find that eight of them indicated, both by actions and words, that they were closer to the new, militant type of Negro leader than to the old, accommodating type. All eight were active in either the local chapter of the NAACP, in a local protest organization, or in both.

Of the four Negro members who seemed to fit the old pattern of leadership, three could be described as in the top level of influence: the college administrator, the laborer, and the county-employed teacher. Their occupations and their relationships to the white community limited the type of leadership they could display. Yet, at the same time, these and other factors gave them significant influence in the Negro community, and even in the white community. The college administrator was undoubtedly restrained by the need to maintain good relations with the white community, which was host to his institution and which contributed financially to it. At the same time, he did not suffer the restrictions he would have if his institution were part of a county or state educational system. A large part of his influence seemed to stem from the importance white leaders in the community attached to his position at the college. The county-employed educator also experienced restraints because of his position. More important to his orientation, however, was a strong identification with the working-class Negroes, many of whom he served in his official capacity. He stated, for example, that he would not use the golf course even when it was possible for him to do so because he feared his participation in this rather expensive hobby would set him apart from the poorer Negroes he served.

There were some significant omissions from the ranks of influential Negroes in the membership of the Committee. Some Negro women cited as leaders were omitted. More significant, so was a

Negro minister known throughout the state as a spokesman for Negroes. He represented the most active and militant type of leadership among Negroes; it was evident that his activities made him a controversial figure even in the Negro community. There was no question that he was regarded by some of the City Commissioners as too radical for an official committee. Perhaps another limitation on his influence locally was the fact that many of his activities were directed toward the county or even state level rather than being community-centered.

## ACTIVITIES OF THE COMMITTEE

During the first year of its existence, the Biracial Committee took only one official action which came to the attention of the entire community and which required a major decision on the part of the Committee. This action, the opening of the municipal golf course to Negroes, was on the agenda at only one meeting. The other meetings were concerned with procedural matters, such as the election of officers, and consideration of the report of the Institute for Social Research.

Segregation of the golf course had been an issue prior to the appointment of the Biracial Committee. At the time the Committee was created, however, the issue was dormant. It had stemmed originally from demands of local Negro golfers that they be permitted to use the course and the threat of a court suit if they were not. At first the issue was resolved by closing the course to white golfers during certain hours of the day and allowing Negroes to play without charge. This arrangement was still in effect when the Committee was created. Shortly after the first meeting of the Committee, however, a group of Negro golfers objected to the fact that they were still being segregated. They requested that they be allowed to play golf on the same basis as white members, including payment of greens fees. The manager of the golf course refused to change the policy, stating that to do so would cause an economic loss to the course through a drastic decrease in white use. He referred the unresolved issue to the City Commission. At this point, however, the Mayor referred the matter to the Biracial Committee, requesting that a decision be reached at its next meeting. From the accounts of members who were present at this meeting, the relationship between the white and Negro members must have undergone more strain than at any other time during the Committee's existence.

Apparently none of the Negro members felt free to oppose the desegregation of the golf course, even if they were inclined to do so. Yet the debate did not center on the basic issue of segregation versus desegregation, nor on the related issue of "gradualism." Instead, some of the white members, seeking to use the Committee as a means of delaying action, fell back on a procedural point. They argued that the Committee was supposed to study any issues referred to it before reaching a decision and would not be proceeding properly if it acted immediately. In spite of their objections, a majority voted to recommend to the City Commission that Negroes be admitted to the golf course on the same basis as whites. Some of the white members openly expressed their displeasure and stated they would submit a minority report objecting to the procedure by which the decision had been reached.

They failed to do so, however, and the manner in which the Committee's recommendation was presented at the open meeting of the City Commission gave the impression that it had been a unanimous recommendation. The Commission promptly voted to accept it and directed the manager of the golf course to comply. The newspaper reported the Committee's action as a unanimous decision and was lavish in its praise of the Committee and the City Commission. No comment was made on the positions taken by individual Committee members during debate of the issue. In addition, the adverse response from individual citizens which some of the white members had feared did not materialize. There was no rash of resignations from the golf club. The dissatisfied white members of the Committee dropped their plan for a minority report protesting the procedure and began taking credit for what was regarded as a constructive act by the Committee. Some of them still felt several months later, however, that the recommendation had been railroaded through the Committee by the manner in which the Mayor presented the issue, and by the alleged bloc-voting of the Negro members.

Later in the year a second issue, concerning seating at the municipal baseball park, almost came before the Committee. As the time for opening the baseball field approached, some Negro fans expressed an intention to demand unsegregated seating in the grandstand during the forthcoming season. The matter was actually placed on the agenda of one Committee meeting. However, a white member, who was also part owner of the local professional baseball team, discussed the matter with the manager of the ball park. They decided that when the season began, Negroes who demanded admission to the main stands instead of the segregated bleachers would be admitted without question. No public statement was made, but when the season opened, Negroes who requested unsegregated seating found they were permitted to buy seats wherever they wished. While this matter did not come before the Committee, a member was instrumental in preventing it from becoming a public issue. Although some members were not aware of this, those who were felt that the Committee should be given credit for resolving this issue.

After the meeting dealing with the golf course, the Committee had no unfinished business pending. Because of the concern of some white members over the procedure followed in that case, however, the Committee asked the Mayor to appear at a meeting the following month and clarify the relationship between the Committee and the City Commission. At this meeting the Mayor left the impression with at least two white members that he felt the City Commission was morally bound to accept any recommendation the Committee made.

No meeting was held the following month. At this time the Institute for Social Research requested permission from the Mayor to meet with the Committee and discuss what it had been doing. The last two meetings of the year, held two months apart, were devoted almost entirely to discussion of the research reports.

## PRESENTATION OF RESEARCH FINDINGS TO THE COMMITTEE

At these meetings, staff members of the Institute for Social Research discussed the community satisfaction survey and presented some of the findings. As indicated above, this procedure had a dual function. First, it was designed to provide a topic of general interest which the members of the Committee might discuss together. Secondly, it enabled representatives of the Institute to observe the relationships of the Committee members to each other. The latter function was served particularly well at the first meeting, when the members were more or less "caught off guard" by the presence of these observers.

The agenda sent to each member with a notice of the meeting

included the report of the Institute for Social Research as one of the items. Remarks of the members as they entered the meeting room indicated, however, that they had no idea what to expect in this report. It appeared to them as simply another routine item of business.

As the members of the Committee entered and took their seats they divided themselves by race, with a few exceptions. There seemed no objection to, or self-consciousness about, the exceptions, however. When the meeting began the tone was very formal. The formality of reading the minutes of the previous meeting plunged the Committee immediately into a rather complicated discussion of procedure. After this was settled the secretary, a Negro member, stated he wished to resign his position because of the conflicting demands of his job. After some confusion over parliamentary procedure, his resignation was accepted, he was elected vice-chairman, and another Negro was elected secretary. A white member was elected assistant secretary.

The significant thing about the business portion of the meeting was the extent of the Negro members' participation in it. It lasted not more than forty-five minutes, as compared to two hours devoted to the subsequent discussion of the Institute's report. During the relatively brief business session the percentage of contributions made by Negroes was at its highest, 39.1 percent; during the remainder of the meeting they made only 20 percent of all contributions. Yet this portion of the meeting was focused not on race relations, the main business of the Committee, but on purely procedural matters.

After the business session the speaker from the Institute for Social Research was introduced. He began with a generalized statement of the nature of the study and the conditions under which the City Commission had authorized it. He emphasized the objectivity of the study and the desire of the research team to gather data from which the Biracial Committee could draw its own conclusions. When a white member asked for further clarification of the purpose of the study, indicating some suspicion of a hidden purpose, the speaker again explained that the study was essentially neutral in nature and that any action taken as a result of the findings would be up to the Committee itself. Then a Negro member, the rather militant lawyer, insisted that any such study must have some sort of value orientation and demanded that the Committee be told what it was. He suggested that the study must have as its purpose the improvement of race reations, or at least a search for factors related to "good race relations" in a community. But for the research team to attempt to define "good race relations" at this stage of the research might very well present the whole research effort in a partisan light, thereby alienating some members of the Committee. Hence the neutrality of the approach was again emphasized.

Although the program lasted two hours, the discussion of the statistical tables presented by the speaker was so lively that it was possible to cover only the objective characteristics of the two samples, white and Negro, including sex, age, education, income, and occupation. At that point the chairman pointed out that the Committee had already met thirty minutes longer than usual, and invited the team to return and discuss the survey at another meeting.

As indicated above, white members were more active in this discussion than the Negro members. A large part of it consisted of expressions of surprise or skepticism at some of the findings, primarily the differentials between the white and Negro samples, followed by speculation as to why they might have turned out as they did. The discussion suggested an important function that might be served by the procedure of presenting survey findings to such a committee. The Negro members did not express the surprise at some of the racial differentials that the white members did, and the questions of the white members gave them an opportunity to make pointed remarks about the status of the Negro in the community. When a white member, a business man, commented, "The Negro needs to balance his representation in business ownership," a Negro member very promptly replied, "You can't do that until you go back to the table showing income levels and raise the Negro's position in that." The white member said, "Yes, it's a question of which comes first." The Negro stated emphatically, "He can't get into the operation of a business until he gets more income to start it with." This sort of incipient attempt by the Negroes to educate the white members was the most significant feature of the discussion of the research findings. Subsequent interviews with individual members revealed that they themselves sensed what was going on and felt it was valuable to the Committee.

The second session with the Committee was held two months later; no meeting had been held during the intervening month. This time the report of the Institute was the only item of business on the agenda. The research team used a somewhat different approach at this meeting, for two reasons. Since good rapport had been established with the Committee at the first meeting, a more direct approach to the topic of the functions of such a committee could be taken. Also, before the meeting the chairman had asked the research team to give the Committee something of a "pep talk" on the importance of what it was trying to do. Therefore one member of the team opened the discussion with a statement concerning the problems of communication between diverse groups in the modern urban community. He explained that the Institute was interested in this community and this Committee because they seemed to be attempting to solve some of their problems of communication. Then he asked the members to comment on whether they felt such a group as theirs could indeed do a long-range job of improving communications between the races, rather than being merely a "fire-fighting team" which functioned only when crises arose. The other member of the research team, in additional comments, suggested an analogy to other community planning committees concerned with such things as housing, zoning, and economic development.

This approach elicited an immediate response. One of the Negro members described how good race relations had been in this community in the past. He said this was because there had always been some method of communication between whites and Negroes, even though it was not always the best method. Then he suggested it was important indeed for the Committee to plan ahead because he could foresee other problems, such as the expansion of Negro housing into previously white areas, which could lead to trouble if not anticipated. A white member then pointed out that this type of committee differed from other planning committees in that other problems did not involve emotions as deep-seated as those related to race relations. He felt adverse public opinion could hinder the work of this committee.

Another Negro warned that complacency about the peaceful nature of race relations in the community could be a danger to the success of this Committee. He argued that an "it can't happen here" attitude could lead to a lack of preparation for the kinds of crises that had occurred in other southern cities such as Montgomery, Birmingham, and New Orleans. Then, in reply to the white speaker's concern about adverse public opinion, he pointed out that the way the newspaper handled the golf course decision, making it appear unanimous, had protected the individual Committee members from reprisals. He suggested that under these circumstances some members would vote for things which they would not individually support if they were exposed to the full force of public opinion.

Another white member, reflecting a frankness which had not been observed in the first meeting, introduced a new theme:

> I am very happy to hear members of the Committee being a little modest about congratulating themselves on the remarkable success of this Committee so far. It has been far from being put to a real test. About all we have done is keep open the lines of communication which have already been in existence, and the very existence of this Committee has come about because that background has been built up through the years.

There was no disagreement with this view, but the Negro member who had first praised the community for its good race relations now expressed optimism that the Committee could actually accomplish something and confidence that it would receive support from the Mayor and the City Commission. He suggested that the present Committee had a better chance of doing something than did the first Biracial Committee, because the first one had some "die-hards" who prevented it from accomplishing anything.

Another Negro stated he felt these factors reflected the type of people who lived in the community, who had, after all, elected the City Commisisoners to office. His expression of pride in the people in the community led the group back to the survey data, with a request for information on comparisons of the people here with people in other Florida communities in such areas as education, occupation, and income. Once again the educational exchange between Negro and white members, which had predominated in the first meeting, began to operate. During the ensuing discussion various Negro members were able to put across the following points, each of which seemed novel to one or more white members: (1) An excess of Negro school teachers existed in the state, in contrast to the shortage of white teachers, due to the greater importance to Negroes of school-teaching as a means of occupational and personal mobility; (2) Negroes had greater difficulty than whites in obtaining financing for such things as home building; (3) Exclusion clauses in certain unions acted as a barrier to occupational opportunities for Negroes in this community.

A tabular presentation which aroused particular interest on the part of both white and Negro members showed that while whites who had migrated to the community were generally less satisfied with it than natives, the reverse was true among Negroes (Table 19). In

TABLE 19

Percent Distribution of Satisfaction Score, by Migration Status

| Satisfaction score | WHITE | | NEGRO | |
|---|---|---|---|---|
| | Migrant | Born in city | Migrant | Born in city |
| 0 (Low) | 8.3 | 10.0 | 19.7 | 32.1 |
| 1 | 5.4 | 5.0 | 7.6 | 3.7 |
| 3 | 3.4 | — | 7.1 | 11.1 |
| 7 | 1.3 | — | 14.3 | 6.2 |
| 15 | 6.2 | 15.0 | 11.3 | 1.2 |
| 31 | 55.8 | 45.0 | 15.2 | 19.8 |
| 63 (High) | 19.6 | 25.0 | 24.8 | 25.9 |
| Total percent | 100.0 | 100.0 | 100.0 | 100.0 |
| Total number | 387 | 20 | 407 | 81 |

the discussion of this table one of the Negro members pointed out that while this community might appear very desirable to a Negro from a much smaller town, it would not appear so good to a Negro who had lived here all his life but found he still "can't do a thing he wants to do." This was the closest approach to a frank protest against the restrictions segregation places on Negroes heard during either of the two meetings. Interestingly, the man making this point was the county employee who has been classified as an accommodating leader.

The final point the Negro members made was related to the relatively high degree of community dissatisfaction expressed by Negroes who had graduated from high school but had not completed college. In this connection, one of the Negro members pointed out that in the community there were trade school and union apprentice programs to fit white high school graduates for a skilled craft, but there was no such training available for Negroes. One of the white members, a school teacher, immediately seized on this as a specific suggestion the Committee might follow up as a means of long-range improvement of race relations in the community.

As the discussion ended, two Negro members appealed for action by the Committee or its individual members. One urged that the Committee not be satisfied with having merely discussed the report but that the members, in their roles as individual citizens and members of other organizations, try to follow through on some of the points brought up in the discussion. The vice-chairman, the Negro college administrator, said he would like the Committee to send a copy of the final report prepared by the Institute to the Mayor and the City Commission with recommendations for investigation of some of the problem areas it disclosed.

In this second meeting the Negro members again took full advantage of the opportunity afforded by the survey findings to explain to the white members some of the disabilities under which their people labored. At no point did any of the white members show signs of resenting statements of this sort or of regarding them as protests. Instead, they seemed to receive them as interesting information they had not possessed before. At the same time, throughout both the sessions, there was a rather careful skirting of the emotionally involved question of segregation. Even when it was pointed out that, in the responses of Negroes to the questions concerning the greatest needs of the community, desegregation of various facilities ranked very low, the Negro members raised no questions and voiced no protest. At the end of the second session the question remained,

Did the Negro members accept these findings as actually reflecting the feeling of their people, or did they wish to avoid raising the controversial issue of segregation?

## NOTES

1. For a more detailed report, see Lewis M. Killian and Charles M. Grigg, "The Biracial Committee as a Response to Racial Tensions in Southern Cities," *Phylon,* 23 (Winter, 1962), pp. 379-82.

2. *Ibid.,* p. 125.

# THREE

# A Biracial Committee
# as Seen by the Members

Approximately one month after this second meeting, a member of the research team interviewed 20 of the Committee members to ascertain their perceptions of the Committee, their reactions to its accomplishments, and their reactions to the presentation of 'the research team. Eleven white and nine Negro members were interviewed. The four remaining members were out of the city while the interviews were being conducted. There were no refusals.

All but one of the subjects were quite willing to be interviewed, and talked freely, and apparently frankly, to the interviewer. None objected to his taking notes. The interviews were conducted in an informal conversational manner. While some specific questions were asked of each subject, the primary technique was to get the subject to talk about the Committee and then to follow up leads he gave in his discussion.

In commenting on the purpose of the Committee, all the members, white and Negro, showed great sensitivity to the specific and somewhat restrictive mandate contained in the ordinance creating the Committee. A majority of them paraphrased that portion of the ordinance which declares that the Committee shall advise the City Commission on matters pertaining to race relations. All were also aware of the fact that the Committee was empowered to make recommendations concerning only those matters the City Commission referred to it.

The members differed, however, in their feelings about these limitations and how far the Committee might possibly go beyond them. The white members tended to accept these limitations as rather restrictive but nevertheless desirable. They felt that they protected the Committee from becoming too active and hence inviting criticism from the white community. They felt the responsibility for any action stemming from a decision of the Committee rested entirely with the City Commission, since only it could make the final decisions.

Two white members, however, interpreted what the Mayor said when he met with the Committee as implying that the City Commission would approve any recommendation the Committee submitted to it. As a result, they perceived the Committee as potentially more powerful and more responsible than did the other members.

## THE BUFFER FUNCTION

Perhaps the main reason the white members approved of the limitations on the Committee was their perception of it as a body designed to be concerned almost exclusively with problems of desegregation. One of them quoted a statement by a political leader who refused to appoint a biracial committee in another city that the only function of a biracial committee was to bring about integration. Another declared, "The purpose of this Committee is to try to alleviate something that is going to happen anyway." Since many of the white members thus felt they were charged with an unpleasant and unpopular task, they were happy that the retention of final authority by the City Commisison gave the Committee some protection. At the same time, some of them saw the Committee as a means of protecting the City Commission. This attitude was expressed in such statements as, "You might say this Committee is a bumping block which protects the City Commission from people who are trying to create issues," and "The biggest purpose is to take problems presented to the City Commission and keep them at the discussion level to keep them from getting into political issues." In general, white members tended to regard the Biracial Committee as a device to permit the white community to delay, through study and discussion, action on requests for desegregation.

## THE PLANNING FUNCTION

Only one Negro member, the conservative county employee, seemed to regard this protective function of the Committee as a valuable one. Six of the Negro members felt that the Committee's restriction to matters referred by the City Commission kept it from doing the job they believed it could and should do. Negro members indicated, both in the interviews and in the two meetings of the Committee, that this body should not wait for problems to arise, but should anticipate and study them before they came to the official attention of the City Commission. One member stated,

> With our limitations it requires some outside group of citizens to bring a problem to the City Commission before the Committee can do anything. This doesn't give the Committee a chance to foresee problems and discuss them before we are confronted with them. As a matter of fact, we don't meet unless there is a problem that confronts the City Commission and has been referred to us.

In other words, the Negro members tended to see the Committee as potentially a planning committee which would take a constructive approach to the whole matter of race relations to the community.

## THE COMMUNICATION FUNCTION

Another function of the Committee, which Negro members emphasized much more than the whites, was communication between the members as representatives of the white and Negro segments of the community. They felt little was being accomplished in this respect, but if the Committee met more often and more informally, it could perform this function effectively. Here again, the Negro members had a broader conception of what a committee of this sort might do than did the whites, who tentatively perceived it as a body designed to meet problems on an *ad hoc* basis.

The chairman was ambivalent about the function and potentialities of the Committee. On the one hand, he was very conscious of the legal restrictions placed on it by the City Commission. Through his actions, he showed no indication of wishing to expand its function. On the other hand, he talked quite expansively about the importance of the Committee. With reference to its function as a channel of communication, he called it a "kind of community summit meeting." With reference to its investigative functions, he compared it to a committee of the U.S. Senate. Furthermore, he felt his position as chairman gave him something of the status of an expert on race relations in the community. He referred to the number of people to whom he had given advice concerning the best posture for the community to assume on problems of desegregation, and he reported he had been asked to expound his philosophy to civic clubs and audiences of teachers in the county. Here he seemed to be suggesting yet another possible function for the Committee, an educational one. Yet except for his personal speaking engagements he apparently had done nothing to implement this goal.

## DESEGREGATION OF THE GOLF COURSE

The one thing which stood out in the minds of all the members as a signal accomplishment of the Biracial Committee was its recommendation for the desegregation of the golf course. All but two members expressed the unqualified feeling that the Committee could indeed be proud of this action. One white member still regarded it as something the Negoes "put over" on the white members, but even he felt the action represented a positive accomplishment. A Negro member played down the importance of the Committee's role in both this case and the informal decision to desegregate seating at the ball park, stating that a great deal of preliminary work had been done in these matters before the Committee ever became concerned with them. In spite of these observations, the Committee's recommendation concerning the golf course, and the way it was received by the City Commission and by the community as a whole, were of great significance to the members. It demonstrated that the white members could make concessions to Negro demands for desegregation without being rejected by the white community, while to the Negro members it showed that the Committee was not just a subterfuge for preventing or delaying any desegregation. To all, it was an example of a potentially explosive community issue being handled calmly and with a minimum of publicity and public controversy. In addition, some of the Negro members felt this decision and its outcome had changed the attitude of many of the white members, particularly the chairman, toward the Committee and their participation on it. The statements of the chairman himself confirmed this. Apparently he felt that this episode had brought him not public disapproval, but a certain amount of glory, which he was still enjoying.

## THE SAFETY VALVE

It is difficult to separate the members' feelings about the accomplishments of the Committee from their feelings about the golf course decision, which seemed to have a halo effect, producing a broad optimism about the strength and potential of the Committee. The other accomplishments cited by members were more general in nature than the golf course and ball park actions discussed above. One was "keeping things calm by giving Negroes a feeling that there was someone to whom they could turn if they were dissatisfied." Two Negro and two white members said they felt the mere existence of the Committee had prevented issues from coming to a head in the community and had kept agitation down. The two Negroes who felt this way were the college administrator and the school teacher, both of whom have been identified as accommodating leaders. Some of the members saw as a second general value the communication that took place in the meetings, although there were as many others, both white and Negro, who felt communication had been rather stiff and limited. Closely related to this was the suggestion by some Negro members that the white members were learning about the viewpoint and the problems of the Negroes.

## PROBLEMS ANTICIPATED BY THE COMMITTEE

The members' uncertainty as to just what the Committee might accomplish was revealed most clearly in their answers to the question, "What problems do you think might come before the Committee in the future?" There was only one problem which a majority of the members, either white or Negro, could cite as likely to be referred to the Committee in the foreseeable future. This was the question of the desegregation of public recreational facilities, particularly the public beach used by tourists. Since any school desegregation would be a county responsibility, the Committee would have no role there, and only one member saw housing for Negroes as a possible issue for the Committee.

Three Negro and two white members could think of no specific imminent problems, and one of these Negroes feared the Committee might become inactive for lack of something to act upon. Thus, because the Committee's essentially crisis-oriented mandate made it difficult for the members to think ahead, the only path most of them could foresee for the Committee led to what was regarded as potentially the most explosive issue in the community—desegregation of the public beach. Their attitude also reflected the implicit assumption of most of the members that the primary, and perhaps only, concern of the Committee was problems relating to desegregation.

Most of the members discussed the question of the beach quite volubly. Those who cited it as an issue that might come before the Committee were asked if they felt the Committee could handle such a controversial matter without becoming hopelessly divided and breaking up. Only one, a white member, felt that such a division might occur.

The white members made it quite clear that they felt this to be the most critical threat to racial harmony in the community. Yet in spite of all expressions of confidence in the Committee, this important topic had never been brought up for discussion. Of course, since the City Commission had not referred it to the Committee, it had not been placed on the agenda for any of the regular business meetings. The topic was also avoided during the two sessions at which the report of the Institute was discussed, even though subjects related to it were considered. These included the low ranking given by Negroes to desegregation as a community need and the large number of Negroes employed in domestic service and other service occupations—questions which could easily have led into the matter of the beach, since a large proportion of the Negro service workers are employed at hotels and motels. The impression was strong that members of the Committee, both white and Negro, were carefully avoiding this important issue.

Individual interviews indicated not only that the beach was an important issue in the minds of the members of the Committee, but also that the white and Negro members tended to perceive the problems differently. The white members viewed the beach as a recreational facility which historically and traditionally had been used exclusively by white people. For Negroes to go there would represent both a break with tradition and a threat to the entire economic structure of the community. None of the white members denied Negroes the legal right to use the beach, since they were aware it was a public recreation area. Rather, they argued that if Negroes availed themselves of this right, tourists from other southern states would object to their presence and would probably take violent action which might lead to fighting, perhaps to a race riot, and certainly to newspaper headlines which would frighten tourists away. The typical white position was that many of the lodging places along the beach were so heavily mortgaged that even a temporary setback in the tourist trade would undermine the economy of the entire community. Two white members spoke vaguely of attempts that had already been made by Negroes to "push their way onto the beach" with reckless disregard of the economic consequences. Interestingly, they ascribed these attempts to Negroes from other communities. It was both a hope and a belief among the white members that local Negroes recognized, as they themselves did, that trouble at the beach would result in unemployment for many Negroes, so that the assertion by a few of their rights would jeopardize the livelihood of many. In general, the white members perceived the problem of the beach as one that could be solved only if the Negroes refrained from asserting their legal rights.

The Negro members recognized the seriousness of the beach issue and accepted the white definition that trouble on the beach would result in economic hardship for all segments of the community. They differed, however, in two important respects. First, seven of the nine Negro members interviewed stated that Negroes already could and did use the beach on occasion. Only one white member had been aware of that fact. Secondly, the Negro members also feared trouble on the beach, but they felt it would arise because the beach police were not taking a strong enough stand against white people harassing Negroes. They reported instances\ in which crowds of whites had gathered around the cars of Negroes picnicking on the beach, throwing sand and making threats. In all cases they felt the police had taken a laissez-faire attitude which tended to encourage rather than discourage the white hecklers. Hence, the Negro conception of a solution to the problem was a firmer stand on the part of the City Commission and the police in defense of the right of Negroes to use the beach. There was no hint of any planned drive by any group in the Negro community to desegregate the beach. As far as they were concerned, the beach was already desegregated, if only on a token basis. Only one Negro, again the county employee, echoed the white viewpoint that Negroes, even local ones, should refrain from going to the beach so as to preserve harmony in the community.

## FUTURE ROLE OF THE COMMITTEE

The general picture, then, was of a committee which felt full confidence in itself because of one successful accomplishment, but which had little idea as to what it could do next. The task which was most evident to the members, that of reducing anxiety about the beach and forestalling trouble there, was one they were avoiding as long as the City Commission did not refer it to them. While some of the members, particularly Negro members, could envisage a broader, more positive approach for the Committee, they had no specific proposals to offer either to the Committee or to the City Commission for a constructive program of action. Hence, at the time of the interviews, the Committee was merely existing and could hardly be described as active. Its primary activity during the preceding four months had been discussing the presentation by the Institute for Social Research.

The Committee members indicated that this presentation did little to reduce their uncertainty as to what they might do. The research report and the discussion of it did suggest that the Committee might have a broader scope and a more constructive approach, but it failed to stimulate any specific suggestions along these lines by Committee members. Three white members and one Negro member gave clearly neutral reactions to the research report. The three white members felt the report failed to be specific in suggesting things the Committee could do, and therefore was of little value. The Negro member agreed, and felt further that the topics discussed were ones that fell more within the province of other agencies. He suggested that since so many of the findings were concerned with economic conditions in the city, such as employment differentials, the report should have been given to the Chamber of Commerce or the Industrial Development Committee. Five white members expressed a rather vague approval of the report and of what the Institute seemed to them to be trying to do, although they did not see anything specific in the report. Only three white members could point to specific values they felt could be derived from the report as they had seen it so far. One felt the discussions had been valuable in demonstrating to the board that a scientific, objective approach to matters of race relations was productive of calm, constructive discussion. Another felt the report had value in pointing out facets of race relations other than problems of desegregation. The third felt it pointed to a need for vocational training for Negro youth, and that this was something the Committee might be able to implement.

With the exception of the one mentioned above, the Negro members were somewhat more enthusiastic in their reaction to the report. They felt it broadened the perspective of the Committee by pointing out new facets of race relations other than segregation. They also suggested that the discussion following the report had helped the relationships between the members of the Committee and had improved communications within that body.

## YEAR-END PROSPECTS

The Committee, as it approached the end of its first year of existence, appeared to have achieved at least a tenous viability. Some of the members, particularly some of the Negro members, saw hopes for positive actions as a planning agency and a channel of communication. Although most of them still had serious reservations about the Committee, the white members perceived it as having a useful function as a safety valve for racial tensions. Feeling that good rapport had been established with the Committee, the research team terminated active intrusion into its activities and stood back to observe possible further developments in its life history. Communication with the chairman was maintained, however, and the Committee was assured at the last joint meeting that the researchers would be "on call" to assist in any way. At the same time, the research team recognized that the Committee did face serious problems. The requirement that it consider officially only matters referred to it by the City Commission did make it difficult for the Committee to develop a program of action on its own initiative. But this very limitation gave the white members a feeling of security they needed in view of their fear of being accused of promoting integration. The quorum rule requiring the attendance of two-thirds of the members of each racial group provided some protection against the threat that either group might "stack the cards" by its more active participation.

At the same time, the requirement that the Committee act only on matters referred by the City Commission forestalled positive action. If the City Commission failed to take a positive approach and initiate action itself, the initiative was most likely to reside in the hands of Negro leaders who would raise issues to be referred to the Committee. This would not only enhance the role of the activist Negro leader, but would also place any Negro member of the Committee in the ambiguous position of virtually being forced to act in the role of an outsider if he wished to bring a matter before the group.

As a result, the main problem of the Committee was to find something to do between crises. A second problem was overcoming the barrier to communication between the white and Negro members, a barrier raised by the fact that the topic uppermost in their minds, desegregation, was the most anxiety-inducing topic.

The community satisfaction survey conducted as the first phase of this research showed that Negroes were indeed concerned with many things besides segregation. It even suggested that desegregation did not have the high priority in the minds of the majority of Negroes that both white and Negro members of the Committee assigned to it. Rather, problems of employment, housing, neighborhood conditions, and the quality of education loomed larger as sources of Negro dissatisfaction. Moreover, these were concerns which Negroes shared to a large extent with their fellow white citizens.

The reaction of the Committee members to the presentation of the research findings showed that broadly oriented research of this kind could suggest, at least for some of the members, a broader perspective on problems of race relations and on possible topics for consideration. In addition, the presentation of the results of objective research for informal, unofficial discussion by the members of the Committee served to facilitate communication between the white and Negro members, providing opportunities for the Negro members to educate the white members on certain aspects of the Negro's situation.

## THE FINAL PHASE: INACTIVITY

This brief experiment did not, however, lead the Committee to initiate any new activity. Nor was there any indication that such new activities would have emerged out of further discussion sessions unless the Board could find both the will and the way to broaden its functions without violating the terms of the ordinance which created it.

The next phase of the history of the Biracial Committee confirmed the impression that presentation of the research findings was an artificial stimulant which served only to prolong the activity of the Committee for a few months. Following the second session of the research team with the Committee, no further meetings were called. About a month after the interviews were completed, the terms of the incumbent members expired. All were reappointed for another year by the City Commission, but over a year later the Committee had yet to meet again. It appeared to be dead, except on paper.

During this entire period, however, the chairman insisted that the Committee was still alive but that things were so quiet that there had been no need for a meeting. "As you know," he said, "we can't meet unless the mayor calls us, and there has been no reason for him to call us." This perception was not one that had been shared by all the members of the Committee, of course, and particularly not by the Negro members. Furthermore, this crisis orientation did not correspond to the emphasis on the planning and communication functions expressed by some of the members.

Race relations had indeed been quiet and peaceful in the sense that there had been no explosive outbreaks. But things had been happening. First of all, during the year that the Committee had been inactive, "token integration" of some white schools in the city had been achieved. This was viewed by the chairman as a "county matter," however, in which a City Board had no reason to become involved. Yet this was one of the potentially explosive developments which a Negro member had suggested, in the last meeting of the board, should be anticipated.

More significantly, a "city matter" had arisen during this period and had been publicly brought to the City Commission. It had not been referred to the Biracial Committee, nor had it been resolved to the satisfaction of the protesting Negroes. The issue concerned the segregation of Negro policemen in the police station through the use of "white" and "colored" signs over the locker-room doors. One of the protesting group declared, "When the inspection was to be made, the signs were taken down. It was handled in the usual way —an expedient way."

Most significant about the episode, however, is the fact that some of the Negro members of the Biracial Committee were prominently involved in lodging the protest! Had the matter been referred to the Biracial Committee, they would have been, in the words of one of them, called on to arbitrate an issue which they themselves had raised.

Yet, surprisingly, this Negro protest leader did not regard the Committee as being "dead" after more than a year of inactivity, any more than the chairman did. And, in spite of the implication in the foregoing account that the chairman and the other white members might, by their inactivity, have been responsible for the cessation of its active career, this Negro member did not place the blame on them. Instead, he said of the Committee,

> It's dormant. It is partly our fault that it hasn't met. We should have asked for a meeting. It was a good thing—it's always good to have communication without hostility to keep the lines of communication open.

When asked if the reason for the inactivity was the fact that there had been no issues, he replied that there were many issues. In addition to the matter of the police station, he enumerated the familiar issue of the beach, the matter of school desegregation, and the problem of employment opportunities. He indicated that the ambiguous situation concerning freedom of Negroes to use the beach remained unchanged. As for the schools, he commented that a suit demanding more than "token desegregation" was still in litigation— "A few Negro children in school doesn't really change things." The problem of employment opportunities had taken on a new aspect, for a new industry was about to open in the community but whether its employment policies would be nondiscriminatory was unclear. In fact, this leader felt that the Negroes may have been "used" by white leaders in inducing the new industry to locate in the city, for he had information that the "good race relations in the city" had been cited as one of its attractions. His characterization of the current situation was,

> There seems to be a "grand design" on the part of the white leadership that keeps anything from happening. Some Negro leaders go along with this grand design. That makes it harder for us, but it doesn't excuse the rest of us for not raising issues.

## DID COOPERATION WORK?

If preservation of an external appearance of "racial harmony" in the community is taken as the measure, this community was successful in preserving good race relations during a period of state-wide and internal tension. Moreover, the Biracial Committee seems to have made some contribution to this success, especially through its "safety-valve" function. But by another measure, that used by the Negro leader quoted above, race relations had not improved significantly during the life of the Biracial Committee. The fundamental problems of the Negro community remained unresolved, affected little by token desegregation of the golf course and the schools. If school desegregation, housing, employment, and use of public recreational facilities had explosive potentialities, these potentialities were still there and no preparation had been made to cope with them. In this sense the cooperative approach symbolized by the Biracial Committee could be deemed a failure. Why?

The Committee existed in a community in which conditions would seem to be optimal for calm, objective consideration of race relations on a biracial basis. It will be recalled that the community was selected as the locus for the research partly because of the absence of racial tension. It is a community characterized by a relatively high level of political participation by Negroes. It was one of the first communities in the state to employ Negro policemen and to hire Negro drivers on city buses. Biracial voluntary associations, church services, and conferences have been held without harassment in the community for several years. Yet the official Biracial Committee played a distinctly secondary role in race relations and within a year of its formation had become inactive.

The Committee developed in the midst of a state-wide crisis in race relations. The existence of a boycott of lunch counters implied the possibility that the sit-in crisis might erupt in the local community. A survey of biracial committees in cities throughout the South indicates that the sense of emergency created throughout the region by the wave of sit-ins was the most important stimulus to the formation of such committees. At the same time, it cannot be assumed that it was simply the threat of sit-ins that led to the formation of the local Committee. The possibility that the appointment of the Committee also reflected the moderate attitude in race relations of the City Commission must not be discounted.

The early activity of the Committee, which was also its only real activity, was related to a minor crisis in the community. This was the threat of Negro golfers to bring suit to change the pattern of segregation which replaced the prior policy of exclusion of Negroes from the municipal golf course. In view of court decisions in other southern cities, white leaders recognized quite clearly that such a suit would probably be successful and that they would be faced with a choice of admitting golfers on an unsegregated basis or closing the golf course. The newly formed Biracial Committee served as a convenient mechanism for resolving the crisis without loss of face. After the crisis had passed, the City Commission found no further use for the Committee and the Committee itself failed to take the initiative in developing its own activities.

One interpretation of the low degree of involvement of this official committee in race relations in the community might be that race relations were so amicable that there was no need for it to be active. Such is certainly the view held by some of the white members, particularly the chairman. Yet the community survey demonstrates that inequalities in the living conditions of whites and Negroes do exist, and that Negroes are subjectively dissatisfied with these inequalities. Both white and Negro members indicated, furthermore, that the virtual exclusion of Negroes from the beach and other recreational facilities, both publicly and privately operated, constitutes a potentially explosive issue which could easily destroy the benign facade of "good race relations." Most of the Negro members indicated their feeling that there was much that the community and the Committee itself might do to improve race relations and the living conditions of the Negro citizens. The more militant members felt that a crisis related to some phase of segregation could arise at any time and that the Committee should be leading the community in preparation for such a crisis. All of the Negro members, and some of the white members, felt that there were enduring inequities in educational opportunity, housing, and employment, which they could, at the least, study. Hence, some other explanation of the failure of the Committee to be more active must be explored.

Although this Committee did not purport to be a cross-section of the community, or even of community leadership, it still may be regarded as a microcosm of the community as it faces the problems of Negro–white relations. The Negro members reflected a variety of attitudes toward minority-group action, from those of the accommodating leader to the militant. The white members, although not representing such a broad range of attitudinal types, reflected in their behavior the inactivity and the "business as usual" posture typical not only of this but of so many communities, particularly in the South. From an analysis of the behavior of this Committee some propositions may be developed as to the conditions under which communities may be expected to act to meet the problems of race relations. At the same time, conclusions may be drawn concerning the probable effectiveness of the biracial committee as a technique of communication.

Reliance on "improving communication" through such a device as the biracial committee implies an ameliorative approach to race relations. To the extent that the committee is expected to bring about change, its function is to stimulate and guide social change through the collaboration of leaders of the white and Negro segments of the community. By the same token, even if it does not itself initiate programs of change, it is expected to forestall conflicts which may arise as the result of demands for change. Race relations are thereby to be taken out of the context of power and placed in the realm of peaceful cooperation. But it is in exactly this respect that such an approach is unrealistic.

What does the analysis of attempts of leaders to engage in interracial communication and cooperation suggest as to why the cooperative, consensual approach is so unproductive of change? One reason that emerges is the reluctance of top-level white leadership to become actively involved in ameliorative efforts—a defect, it may be recalled, which was pointed out by McKee in his critique of *A Manual of Intergroup Relations*. Analysis of the career of the Biracial Committee in a Florida city supported McKee's proposition. It has been shown that, by their own definition, the majority of the white members were not from the top echelon of influential citizens in the community. Some of the more influential but also more conservative leaders had been on the first Biracial Committee; they had hastened its demise by their adamant defense of the status quo. One of the most influential of these conservative leaders had been asked to serve on the new Committee and had declined. The orientation to the general white power structure of those white leaders who were on the Committee, and their fear of sanctions for going too fast for both the most influential leaders and the white community in general, were evident. As McKee suggested would be the case, their orientation was fundamentally toward preserving the status quo. While even the most conservative members recognized that change would come about in the community as a result of Negro pressure, they perceived their function as that of containing the force of the Negro pressure and at the same time protecting the community from undesirable publicity or economic loss.

## WHITE AND NEGRO PERSPECTIVES

A second proposition is, that like most white Americans, even those white leaders who attempt to communicate and cooperate with their Negro counterparts do not see racial inequality in the same way that the Negro does. The white person, no matter how liberal he may be, exists in the cocoon of a white-dominated society. Living in a white residential area, sending his children to white schools, moving in exclusively white social circles, he must exert a special effort to expose himself to the actual conditions under which large numbers of Negroes live. Even when such exposure occurs, his perception is likely to be superficial and distorted. The substandard house may be overshadowed in his eyes by the television aerial or the automobile outside the house. Even more important, he does not perceive the subjective inequalities inherent in the system of segregation because he does not experience them daily as a Negro does. Simply stated, the white American lives almost all of his life in a white world. The Negro American lives a large part of his life in a white world also, but in a world in which he is stigmatized.

One of the explicit goals both of biracial committees and community surveys is to improve communication and thereby make representatives of the white community more nearly aware of the objective living conditions as well as the subjective reactions to Negroes to their status. In this study, the presentation of survey findings to the Biracial Committee and the stimulating of discussion of these findings were designed to ascertain if this greater comprehension of the other viewpoint would be achieved. Although two of the white members of the Board did indicate, both in the discussion and in the interviews, that they received more new insights, the majority of the white members revealed little change in their perception, and even less inclination to do anything about the situation. It has been pointed out that one white member implied that not joint community action but self-improvement by Negroes was what was needed.

Herman Long has described this kind of reaction of white representatives, suggesting that it is typical of the dominant and power elements of the community.

> They are inclined to minimize the degree of lack of equal opportunity though ready to admit its possibility, but most importantly they proceed with the basic orientation and assumption that the lack of such opportunity in jobs, housing, and even public accommodations can be attributed to the general inadequacy on the part of the minorities themselves.[1]

In contrast Long suggests,

> Within this same context of community-wide leadership effort, minority group leaders involved in the relationship are inclined to assume a different and much simpler form of causation, namely discrimination.[2]

This very well describes the reaction of most of the Negro leaders on the Biracial Committee. Although they did not say so in the Committee discussions, in interviews they displayed concern about many areas of discrimination in their apparently peaceful city. They felt the survey findings pointed up the existence of inequalities. Their desire for positive action, as well as their impatience over the unlikelihood of the Biracial Committee's taking any such action, was reflected in the difference in their perception of the potential of the Committee and the perception which the whites had. One of the more conservative Negro representatives on the Committee took an optimistic view and proposed, in the last session, that the Committee should take positive action to bring the survey findings before the entire community for discussion. But the more militant Negro members perceived the restrictive provisions of the Committee's charter and the obvious reluctance of the white members to initiate change as insurmountable obstacles to effective action. Their appraisal of the situation proved to be the more realistic one for, in the absence of issues raised through the application of power, the Committee not only failed to act, but ceased to meet. Most significantly, the Committee, even during its period of activity, never addressed itself to the problem uppermost in the minds of both white and Negro members as the most explosive issue in the community. This was the use of the beach by Negroes.

In spite of the existence of the Committee, the community, like many southern communities, remained in a state of uneasy equilibrium. The thing most likely to disturb this equilibrium was the very thing that the Committee was designed in part to prevent, the resort to force by Negroes outside the Committee. The "force" that was feared was a wade-in or some other type of demonstration designed to assert the legal right of Negroes to use a public recreation facility without interference. That this type of force might be used, with a consequent violent reaction by segments of the white community, was fully recognized by both white and Negro leaders. Some of the white leaders were convinced, in fact, that there was already a Negro "plot" to force the desegregation of the beach. The Negro leaders knew that there had already been incidents in which white hecklers had interfered with Negroes who attempted to use the beach unobtrusively, not as part of a demonstration. Yet the Committee carefully avoided discussion of this issue and proposed no action to meet it.

## BARRIERS TO COMMUNICATION:
### THE RULE OF CHARITY

A third proposition may be advanced to explain the avoidance of what seems to be a crucial issue in race relations: The very emphasis on communication and cooperation implied in the formation of a biracial committee serves to inhibit free discussion. In the meetings of the Biracial Committee, what Long has called "the rule of charity," clearly operated. He argues,

> In community projects geared toward involving a "balance" of different leadership elements in which involving elements of the community "power structure" has become a strategic goal the differences in dominant and minority group definitions of the reasons for the existence of inequality of opportunity becomes crucial. There is in these instances the operation of what has been called a rule

of charity, whereby the groups, recognizing their basic difference in interest and orientation, refuse to bring to the fore matters which might either embarrass the other or widen the already existing political and socio-psychological distance between them.[3]

The very nature of the community biracial committee, designed to bring together representatives of the power structures of the white and Negro subcommunities, is such that it is not likely to be an effective agent for bringing about discussion of the most tension-laden issues.

Still it would seem that the biracial committee, to the extent that it includes militant Negro leaders, should provide an arena in which there can be a confrontation of white leaders with the power of the Negro community, rather than with the force represented by the actual application of sanctions. In another short-lived biracial committee, a militant Negro member attempted to bring the power of the minority community to bear in just such a way. His technique was to remind the white members repeatedly that he could hold his people in check only so long as the committee was doing something. He found, however, that this technique met with very limited success.

## LIMITATIONS OF "THE BIRACIAL TEAM"

A fourth proposition suggests why the power of the Negro subcommunity does not serve as a dynamic force moving a biracial leadership group to action: A latent function of a biracial leadership group is to inhibit the exercise of power by the Negro leaders who participate. As members of a biracial committee, particularly one with official standing, they are not in a position to apply the power of the Negro subcommunity effectively. In analyzing their anomalous position we may use Erving Goffman's concept of "the team." When they are included on such a committee they cease to be simply representatives of conflicting subcommunities but become members of a team which represents the entire community. But in a team, as Goffman points out,

> Instead of a rich definition of the situation, reality becomes reduced to a thin party line, for one may expect the line to be unequally congenial to the members of the team.[4]

Since, as has been suggested, the Negro and white members of the committee come as representatives of subcommunities with fundamentally different goals, the narrowing of the definition of reality becomes even more imperative since the bonds holding the team together are already so tenuous. The party line, of which Goffman speaks, might also be viewed as a superordinate goal which the different members of the team must accept if the team is to function at all.

It is quite clear that since the definitions of the problem of intergroup relations held by white and Negro members are fundamentally different and conflicting, the resolution of the moral issue cannot serve as this superordinate goal or "party line." McKee argues that Dean and Rosen assume that the moral problem has been resolved even for conservative community leaders, in that they assert that "being for good intergroup relations is like being against sin." [5] The responses of mayors and city managers to the question of why their communities appointed official biracial committees seem to suggest that "good race relations" or "improving race relations" does indeed constitute an acceptable goal, this being the most frequently cited reason for the appointment of such committees. Semantics are crucial at this point, however. To whites, whether liberal or conservative, "good race relations" may mean simply the gradual correction of obvious inequalities, the absence of glaring injustices, and most important, the absence of physical conflict and a sense of crisis in the community. Particularly since 1954, these things do not constitute "good race relations" to Negroes. Louis Lomax has pointed out that not even white liberals perceive race relations in the same way that Negroes do. He comments,

Through the liberal eye, things are better than they were in, say, 1950, and he cannot understand why the courageous Negro leadership organizations that have played such a magnificent role in the past decade are now under bitter and open attack.[6]

## THE SUPERORDINATE GOAL: "RACIAL PEACE"

But Negro leaders, with the exception of a few of the most militant, do not desire racial conflict, nor are they unwilling to accept an atmosphere of harmony in the community as a goal. Their will-

ingness to support and serve on a biracial committee reflects the
hope that change may come about in the community without the
ordeal of nonviolent resistance and demonstrations, with all the risks
that they entail. Hence, *the preservation of racial peace* becomes the
superordinate goal for which both white and Negro members of the
biracial committee can work. But this creates a serious dilemma for
the Negro leader, particularly the militant leader who, if forced to,
would choose progress over peace. The dilemma arises from the
fact that peace does not serve as an effective superordinate goal
*unless there is some threat to this peace.* The Negro leader cannot
simultaneously serve as a guardian of the peace of the community
and at the same time threaten this peace by invoking the power of
the Negro community. The more militant Negro leaders on the Committee under consideration here recognized this. One of them pointed
out that the Committee operated in such a way that it could take no
action unless an issue was created in the community to be referred
to the Board. If the leader who is on the biracial committee takes
the leadership in creating such an issue he is likely to be rejected
as a member of the team by the white members because he has vio-
lated the "rule of charity." This threatens the very existence of the
committee, because his fellow Negro members are then placed in
the position of joining the whites in their rejection of him or of
drawing together as a solid racial bloc in his defense, thereby alienating themselves from the white portion of the team. The other alternative is for the Negro members of the committee to relinquish
the dynamic leadership role in the Negro community to people outside the committee. If they themselves represent the top leadership
in the Negro community, this means that they leave the field open
for reckless parvenues who may, for a variety of reasons, be anxious
to challenge their position. Furthermore, when issues created by
such free-lance leaders do come before the committee for resolution,
the established leaders whose job it is to negotiate may appear in
the role of the Uncle Tom who does not negotiate with whites, but
compromises in slowing down change to a pace acceptable to the
white power structure. But, again, if the Negro member of the committee refuses to negotiate, but instead supports whatever Negro
demands come before the team, he takes the risk of destroying the
cooperative venture. In optimistically accepting the flattering and
seductive premise that, as a member of a biracial committee he be-

comes a partner with the white leader in a generalized community leadership, the Negro leader eschews his role as an antagonist in a power struggle.

Ironically, the more the white representative on such a body sympathizes with the plight of the Negro team member and defines racial problems in the same terms as do the Negro leaders, the more he finds himself confronted with a similar dilemma. In this community and others, city officials have had difficulty persuading white leaders to serve on such boards because they feared that the mere fact of membership might cause them to be branded by their fellow whites as "integrationists." If the white leader, having agreed to serve, advocates change in race relations without a prior application of power by the Negro minority, he may be perceived by both his fellow white members and by his peers in the white community as having failed to support the white interests which it is supposed to represent.

The conservative orientation of powerful white leaders and its debilitating effect on the biracial committee and intergroup cooperation have been examined. But Negro leaders and white liberals, although excluded from the top power group, are still important actors in community race relations. Many observers have placed great hope in the alliance of these two groups as the force which might move the South in the direction of real racial equality without splitting the regional society into two hostile camps, one all-white and the other all-Negro, sharing formal equality but lacking love. Thompson observed of New Orleans,

> Some leaders are convinced that racial desegregation in that city depends heavily upon the extent to which all types of Negro leaders and white liberals find common grounds for cooperation.[7]

Myrdal's belief was that, because of the potency of the American Creed, the Negroes' greatest source of aid is to be found among their apparent antagonists, the white dominant groups. He declared,

> The Negroes are a minority, and they are poor and suppressed, but they have the advantage that they can fight wholeheartedly. The whites have all the power, but they are split in their moral personality. Their better selves are with the insurgents. The Negroes do not need any other allies.[8]

Essential to the analysis of the prospects for interracial cooperation, therefore, is an examination of the trends in Negro leadership
and of the role of the white liberal. A study of Negro leadership
during and after a crisis in another Florida city suggests that the
situational pressures on Negro leaders are making such cooperation
increasingly difficult. Analysis of the position of the white liberal
suggests some of the reasons for what Thompson called "the retreat
of the Liberals." [9]

## NOTES

1. Herman Long, "Community Research and Intergroup Adjustment," in
J. Masuoka and P. Valien, eds. *Race Relations: Problems and Theory* (Chapel
Hill: The University of North Carolina Press, 1961), p. 275.

2. *Ibid.*

3. *Ibid.*

4. Erving Goffman, *The Presentation of Self in Everyday Life* (Garden
City, New York: Doubleday Anchor Books, 1959), p. 85.

5. McKee, *op. cit.,* p. 197.

6. Louis Lomax, *The Negro Revolt* (New York: Harper & Row, Publishers, 1962), p. 5.

7. Thompson, *op. cit.,* p. 170.

8. Myrdal, *op. cit.,* p. 1003.

9. Thompson, *op. cit.,* p. 161.

# FOUR

# Negro Protest Leaders
# in a Southern Community

One of the significant features of race relations in recent years has been the emergence of new patterns of Negro leadership in southern communities. Prior to the various court decisions that withdrew legal support from the traditional framework of segregation, Negro leadership gave the appearance of conforming to the pattern of "accommodating" or "compromise" leadership. Analyses of leadership in southern Negro communities, such as the treatment found in Myrdal's *American Dilemma,* suggest that the compromise leaders held their positions primarily because they were acceptable to white leaders. They were also accepted by Negroes because accommodation was regarded as the most practical and effective mode of adjustment in the existing power situation. Thompson explained the historical effectiveness of the accommodating leader or Uncle Tom in these terms:

> Most of the favors the Uncle Toms receive are due to the fact that in order to be serviceable to the white community, they must maintain prestige among Negroes. They must, therefore, evince some influence with white authorities. *This the white community understands.* (Italics ours)[1]

But, he adds,

> The Uncle Tom is fundamentally a preserver of a biracial system which perpetuates white paternalistic men of power in their status as hosts and Negroes as parasites.[2]

The desegregation decisions of the U.S. Supreme Court, even without extensive implementation, redefined the power situation in which the accommodating leader functioned most effectively. In the years following 1954 militant leaders, reflecting the protest motive instead of the theme of patience and accommodation, have moved into the focus of attention of both whites and Negroes. Whereas the accommodating leaders had not been widely known to the white public, largely because they operated in a noncontroversial and often clandestine manner, the new leaders quickly rocketed to fame or notoriety, depending upon the observer's point of view. Martin Luther King, defying the white power structure of his community and being featured on the cover of *Time* magazine, symbolizes this new leadership. Many white leaders have reacted by bewailing the "breakdown of communication" between the races, denouncing the militant Negro leaders as reckless, radical parvenues, and attempting to isolate them by parleys with handpicked, "responsible" leaders.

Thompson found that just such a "breakdown" did occur in New Orleans, declaring,

> The more or less abrupt departure of the Uncle Tom from the leadership scene has left top white officials with almost no reliable line of communication with Negro leaders.[3]

In one north Florida community a change in the pattern of Negro leadership accompanied a crisis in race relations. The critical situation arose from a challenge to segregation on city buses, culminating in a boycott. Here, too, news media featured daily the names of militant Negroes who previously had been anonymous ciphers in the Negro community as far as most whites were concerned. There were allegations that "newcomers" had come into the community and stirred up the erstwhile contented population and that the Negro leadership had "split" with the result that white leaders did not know with whom to deal. Hence this community was well suited for a case study of Negro leadership in the present era of tension.

The situation provided an opportunity to get the answers, for this community, to the question:

Was the leadership in this protest movement actually new to the Negro community, or were the new leaders merely people who had suddenly become known to the white community because of a change of strategy? If they were new to the higher levels of the power structure in the Negro community, had they actually displaced the old group of leaders or was the community split between two competing sets of leaders? Did these "new leaders" draw their strength from popular support or simply from a tightly organized, activist minority?

## METHOD OF STUDY

The study, executed shortly after the end of the bus boycott, consisted of two related parts. The first was an assessment of the structure of Negro leadership through interviews with a panel of 21 Negroes tentatively designated as "leaders" by social scientists familiar with the community. This list subsequently proved to include what came to be defined as "old" and "new" leaders in almost equal proportions.

A panel of 21 white leaders who had dealt with the Negro community in connection with the bus protest, or were known to have worked directly with the Negro community in connection with other matters, was also interviewed. They were the white leaders who most often spoke to the Negro community in behalf of the white community. Some of them were high in the power structure. That this group indeed represented the position of the white leadership in the community was indicated by the absence of opposition to the way in which they dealt with the Negro community.

The names of the 21 Negroes tentatively listed as "leaders" were placed on a card which was handed to the subject during the interview. Then he was asked a series of questions about Negro leadership before and after the bus boycott, and told to respond by giving names from the list. The questions which are of interest here were:

1. As best you can recall, which would you have identified as "leaders" among Negroes two years ago?
2. At that time, which do you feel were able to influence large numbers of Negroes on important public issues?
3. Which ones were able to express most accurately the feelings of most Negroes on important public issues?
4. Which ones were able to deal most effectively with white leaders as representatives of the Negro group?
5. Now, at the present time, which do you feel are most able to influence large numbers of Negroes on important public issues?
6. Which are able to express most accurately the feelings of most Negroes?
7. Which are able to deal most effectively with white leaders?

Subjects were allowed to give as few or as many responses to each question as they wished, and Negro subjects were encouraged to include their own names if they felt they should.

After the data had been collected, the answers of white and Negro informants were tabulated separately. Each of the 21 potential Negro leaders was given a score and a rank on each question, according to the number of times his name was mentioned in response to the question. Hence each Negro had, for each question, a rank assigned him by the Negro informants and a rank assigned by the white leaders.

The second portion of the study was an attitude survey of a sample of the adult Negro population. Every fifth address was taken from a list of all the households in blocks occupied only by Negroes. Any adult available at the address was interviewed. A total of 196 usable interviews was obtained. A Likert-type scale of statements concerning attitudes toward segregation in general, the bus boycott, and the leadership of the bus protest movement was used. Key items for purposes of this study were:

1. The Negro should not boycott to achieve his goals. (Agreement with this statement would represent a repudiation of the militant leaders.)
2. The old, established leaders were more effective than the ones leading the bus protest.
3. The leadership in the bus protest is very good.

Subjects were grouped into three categories on the basis of whether their answers to these three items reflected approval or disapproval of the leaders who had called for the bus boycott. Those who responded favorably to all three of the statements were classified as "Highly favorable," those who responded favorably to two were classified as "Favorable," and those who responded favorably to only one or none were placed in the "Unfavorable" category.

## THE OLD LEADERSHIP AND THE NEW

The interviews with the panel of potential Negro leaders revealed that a real change in leadership had indeed taken place between the "pre-boycott" and "post-boycott" periods. On the basis of high rankings on the answers to the questions "Who were the leaders?" "Who were influential?" and "Who were representative?" two years previously, six individuals were classified as "pre-boycott leaders." Of these six, not one was found in the first five ranked on "influence" and "representativeness" in the post-boycott period. None of them was ranked even in the first ten on "influence," and "representativeness" in the post-boycott period, and not one was among the first ten named as "leaders" in the post-boycott period.

This change of leadership was also found to involve, as had been postulated, a replacement of accommodating leaders by protest leaders. Of the six pre-boycott leaders, five were ranked by Negroes as being most able to deal effectively with white leaders during this period. Five of the six were also ranked by whites as most able to deal effectively with white leaders. Four, including the three ranked highest by Negroes as "leaders," were ranked in the first five as "emissaries" by both Negroes and whites. This finding bears out the theory that, in the era of accommodation in race relations, leadership in the Negro community was based primarily on acceptability to white leaders and ability to gain concessions from them.

In contrast, none of the five "new leaders" was ranked by either Negroes or whites among the five Negroes able to deal most effectively with white leaders in the post-boycott period. In fact, none of them ranked in the first ten on acceptability to white leaders as it was perceived by Negroes. Clearly these new leaders were not seen by other prominent Negroes as "compromise leaders."

The panel of Negroes interviewed included both the "old leaders" and the "new leaders," plus some individuals who did not receive high ranking for either period. The Negro panel was divided, for purposes of further analysis, into an "old group" of subjects who had ranked in the first ten on the question concerning pre-boycott leadership, and a new group. The new group identified as the five most influential leaders in the post-boycott period the same five men who had been ranked as "new leaders" by the entire panel. The "old group" ranked four of these five men as the five most influential leaders in this same period, indicating that their perception of the change in leadership was almost the same as that of the "new group." Moreover, none of the "old group," including the "old leaders," gave their own names in response to the question on ability to influence large numbers of Negroes. Although during the course of the boycott some of the old leaders had openly challenged the influence of the new leaders, by the time of this study they seemed to have accepted the fact that they had been displaced. It is accurate, therefore, to say that a change, not a split, in leadership had occurred.

Although no intensive study of the individual characteristics of the old and new leaders was made, certain traits were evident. Even though at the time of the study the boycott had ended and had obviously failed in its purpose of forcing desegregation of city buses, all of the new leaders were strongly identified with it. All were officers of the organization that had led the boycott and all had been arrested and fined for "operating an illegal transportation system" (a car pool). In contrast, not one of the old leaders had been active in promoting the boycott, and at least two of them had opposed it as a tactic. Of the six old leaders, three were employed in the state-supported school system; none of the five new leaders was a state employee. There were three ministers among the new leaders, none among the old. Although the old leaders, as a group, had indeed lived in the community a longer time than their successors, the shortest time that any of the new leaders had lived there was three years. One of them had lived there over thirty years. It was only in a limited and relative sense that they could be described as "newcomers."

Since the new leaders had been identified as synonomous with the leaders of the bus boycott, the items used in the opinion poll were suited to serve as a measure of their popular support. When asked if the leadership in the bus protest was very good, 84 percent of the sample agreed that it was. Some inconsistency was found between the responses to this item and the statement, "The old established leaders were more effective than the ones leading the bus protest," since only 62 percent disagreed with this statement. To the extent that this sample can be taken as representative, it appears that the new leaders did have majority support in the Negro community. Subjects were also asked to agree or disagree with the statement, "Should the Negro population need to develop united action to obtain rights or services not connected with the bus protest, the people leading the protest would probably be selected to lead such action." Again, strong majority support of the new leaders was indicated, 82 percent of the sample agreeing with this statement.

## SIGNIFICANCE OF THE SHIFT IN LEADERSHIP

The impression that there had been a change in the quality of race relations was borne out. The clearest indication of this change was the replacement of the old leaders by new leaders who clearly reflected the protest theme rather than any spirit of accommodation. These new leaders had widespread popular support, and the extent of their influence was conceded by the old leaders whom they displaced.

Additional findings lent added significance to this shift in Negro leadership. The panel of white leaders was found to perceive Negro leadership in the post-boycott period in almost the same way that the Negro leaders did. Of the six men ranked highest by whites as "most influential" in the post-boycott period, four were among the Negroes' new leaders. At the same time, most of the white leaders indicated that they were unwilling to deal with these new leaders because the militant spokesmen were uncompromising in their opposition to segregation. It is only in this sense that communication had broken down between the races. The new leaders were unwilling to communicate and negotiate with whites in the circumscribed, accommodating fashion of yesterday. The old leaders could no longer claim the support of the Negro population, no matter how acceptable they might be to the whites. As long as this situation prevailed, the structure of the situation seemed to permit only one kind of communication between the Negro community and the white power structure: formal, peremptory demands, backed by the threat of legal action, political reprisal, or economic boycott. So long as the new leaders were not accepted as bona fide, albeit antagonistic, emissaries of the Negro community in the same way that the old leaders were, this would seem to be the only way in which they could get the attention of the white leaders.

While this study was principally concerned with a description of the changes in Negro leadership during the bus protest, there is evidence that indicates that the new leaders and new leadership are permanent in this community. Although they may have been "issue leaders" at first, they have continued to maintain their position of leadership as the sample of the Negro population predicted they would.

In the first place some of the "old" leaders were called upon by the City Commission to get the Negroes to agree to a compromise settlement in the early days of the bus protest. The efforts of the "old" leaders to do this failed completely, and since then they have made no overt efforts to regain the following they had prior to the bus protest, believing that neither the Negro population nor the city officials have confidence in them. The Negroes do not trust them because of what they regard as underhanded dealing with the City Commission. The city officials apparently feel that these erstwhile leaders cannot be trusted to gauge Negro sentiment accurately or to deliver results when called upon because they lack following.

Secondly, the "new" leaders have continued to enjoy reasonable support for their undertakings. Some of them have moved into other areas of leadership, such as the NAACP, the Southern Christian Leadership Conference, and the Florida Council of Human Relations. One of them is president of the local chapter of the NAACP. Another is on the state NAACP board and on the Board of Directors of the Southern Christian Leadership Conference.

Finally these "new" leaders have sought to keep the Negro community militant and dynamic by continuing weekly meetings of the organization formed to promote the bus protest, conducting institutes on nonviolence, taking preliminary steps toward school integration, working to get more Negroes registered and voting, and making many local and nonlocal public appearances in connection with the uplift of Negroes. Furthermore, the press had done much to contribute to their status as permanent leaders by seeking their opinions and comments on various matters affecting the Negro community.

The "new" leaders are becoming permanent leaders not because of the attractiveness of their personalities or their skill at organizing, but rather because they adhere rigorously to the form of militant leadership which is becoming the trend for Negroes throughout the United States. This new leadership is not of the accommodating type. It seeks gains for the Negro community through formal demands and requests, boycotts, lawsuits, and voting. The protest leaders are not concerned with whether or not the whites high in the power structure know, like, or want to deal with them. Until the "old" leaders are willing or able to translate their mode of leadership into a form similar to this, it appears that they will not again rise to prominence as leaders.

But it is not only the erstwhile accommodating leaders who are under pressure to give proof of their militancy. Thompson postulates an intermediate type, "the racial diplomat" who does not accept segregation as does the Uncle Tom but may compromise on the issues of segregation in order to secure other gains. He, too, experiences the pressure, for, "The racial diplomat is often hated by other Negro leaders because there is always a feeling of suspicion on their part that he 'sells out to white people.' " [4]

Most significant for the prospects of cooperation and negotiation, however, are the indications that even the protest leader, the "race man," may be under pressure to adopt increasingly extreme modes of militancy. It is clear now that the sit-in movement of 1959-1960 was an indictment of the NAACP for "going too slow." These demonstrations were a forcible reminder even to the "new" Negro leaders that the impatience of their followers was such that the movement would not be allowed to slacken its pace. No matter how great his past accomplishments, if a leader did not produce new examples of progress, even more militant leaders would arise. Since that time, the Black Muslims have risen to prominence, warning of the possibility of even more militant, perhaps violent forms of protest. In the words of Eric Lincoln:

It is not necessary to argue the possibility of a black nationalist putsch in America, but it is fruitful to look at the facts. The world is in social revolution and the Negroes in America are part of that revolution. The student movement, Martin Luther King's movement, the new militancy in the churches, the mushrooming cults of black nationalism which keep springing up in the *Black Ghettoes* of our great industrial cities, are all shades of protest in a revolutionary spectrum.[5]

Daniel Thompson suggests, on the basis of his New Orleans study, that there are at least three basic race-relations leadership patterns, paralleling the spectrum of Negro leadership types. Segregationists, he suggests, prefer to work through Uncle Toms, white moderates can work with racial diplomats, while only white liberals can work effectively with the race man.[6] It is the race man, however, who is becoming increasingly significant as the spokesman for the Negro. Communication between white leaders and Uncle Toms had broken down because of its ineffectiveness, and the effectiveness of the racial diplomat is increasingly threatened. Examination of the position of the white liberal vis-à-vis the broadening of the spectrum of Negro leadership suggests that even communication between him and the "race man" may be losing its significance.

## NOTES

1. Thompson, *op. cit.*, p. 63.
2. *Ibid.*
3. *Ibid.*, p. 167.
4. *Ibid.*, p. 70.
5. C. Eric Lincoln, "Extremist Attitudes in the Black Muslim Movement," *New South* (Atlanta: Southern Regional Council), 18 (Jan., 1963), p. 8.
6. Thompson, *op. cit.*, p. 78.

# FIVE

# The Role of
# the White Liberal

Tremendous importance has been ascribed to white liberals as an actual or potential force in changing patterns of race relations in the South. Yet there is no group whose role in the historical processes of the past eight years has been more ambiguous.

Southern liberals have been held up as evidence that the white South is not indeed "solid." There has been the implication that they constitute the embryo of a new southern leadership which will, as the futility of resistance to desegregation becomes increasingly evident, assume the mantle of leadership. In describing the American race problem as a problem in the hearts and minds of white men, Myrdal suggested that the southern liberal might yet play a significant role in the solution of the American dilemma. Committed to the general valuations of the American Creed as opposed to the specific valuations of the regional ethos, he is a visible reminder of the conflict of values among and within white Americans.

At the same time, Myrdal concluded that southern liberals were a political minority with little power and small expectation of soon achieving power. Because of this lack of power, he observed,

> . . . The southern liberal . . . has become inclined to stress the need for patience and to exalt the cautious approach. . . . In their activities southern liberals have developed the tactics of evading principles; of being very indirect in attacking problems; of cajoling, coaxing, and luring the public into giving in on minor issues.[1]

But even when the white liberal is silent and inactive he is still considered important. Sympathetic observers view him hopefully as representative of the modern "silent South," which soon will speak and cast a deciding vote in the contest between the Negro protest and southern resistance. Less sympathetic observers, usually from outside the region, regard the great majority of southern liberals as the greatest of sinners because they have done so little when presumably they could have accomplished so much. Even the most adamant leaders of the resistance movement attach great significance to the role of the southern liberal. Speaking of "moderates" in the South, a southern governor declared,

> [The northern press] keeps telling us that if all of us segregationists would shut up, then the "moderates" could sneak in and take over, and everything down South would be fine. These moderates we've been hearing so much about are nothing more than southern burglars. They want to rob us of our priceless heritage. . . .[2]

A special wrath is reserved for the white liberal, even though he be "moderate." He is viewed as the white man who has broken the solid front of resistance to the demands of Negroes. He is regarded as the traitor but for whom the battle would have been won.

## DEFINITION OF THE WHITE LIBERAL

The significance attached to the southern white liberal, and the strong emotions he arouses, render objective analysis of his role exceedingly difficult. Before undertaking the task it is necessary to define what is meant by "the southern liberal" at a time when the term "liberal" is itself a source of much confusion. In the context of race relations the term is less confusing, however. The white liberal is, very simply, the white man who has rejected segregation and the categorical inferiority of the Negro as values. He may be a gradualist, or he may believe in the necessity for an immediate, direct attack on the existing pattern of segregation. But, however, he may differ from his fellow liberals as to means, he believes that the old order should and will change. In Myrdal's terms, he is aware of the tension produced between general valuations and specific valuations, and he believes he should work toward the application of the ideals of the American creed to all Americans, including Negroes.

## INDIVIDUAL ATTITUDES AND SOCIAL NORMS

The white liberal has been defined here in terms of attitudes, whether privately held or publicly expressed. It must be recognized.

however, that the individual with these attitudes functions as part of a society characterized by a social structure and a normative order which are not merely reflections of the discrete attitudes of the individuals who make up the society. The normative order is a reflection of what Herbert Blumer has called "the sense of group position." He says,

> . . . The sense of group position is a norm and imperative—indeed, a very powerful one. It guides, incites, cows, and coerces. . . . This kind of sense of group position stands for and involves a fundamental kind of group affiliation for the members of the dominant racial group. To the extent that they recognize themselves as belonging to that group they will automatically come under the influence of the sense of position held by that group. . . . The locus of race prejudice is not in the area of individual feeling but in the definition of the respective positions of the racial groups.[3]

The social structure and the normative order do not change as readily as do individual attitudes, for they are products of the constant interaction between public behavior, reflecting the definition of group position, and private attitudes. Overt compliance may occur without private acceptance of the norms. This differential is a source of both stability and change in a society. The conformity of "fair-weather illiberals" with norms prohibiting discrimination may lead to change. But it should also be remembered that the conformity of fair-weather liberals serves to perpetuate the status quo.

Opinion polls and attitude surveys show that attitudinal support for discrimination against Negroes is far from being unanimous and unequivocal. But analysis on the sociological level must lead to the conclusion that throughout the United States, and particularly in the South, the social structure and the normative order support the inferior social status of the Negro. The many desegregation decisions of the federal judiciary notwithstanding, many formal norms still confirm this inferior position. There are many legal supports for segregation and discrimination which have not been tested in the courts and which, in spite of the general spirit of recent court rulings, remain the law of the land. The informal norms consign the Negro to segregated and usually inferior residential areas, to the lower levels of the occupational ladder, to positions of relatively minor political influence, and to a separate social life. This is not the result of a rational, conscious choice by the members of the society, but is the product of a historical, socio-cultural process. Although most people, if challenged, may express an attitude favorable or unfavorable to one or several of the many practices in race relations, they do not go around thinking constantly about this pattern and its consistency with their values. Instead, they accept it as the normal order of things and operate easily and comfortably within it, as within any cultural framework. Most southern white people, including many southern liberals, act as if race relations are "good" as long as the relationships between people are peaceful and there is no crisis. The increasing depersonalization of relations between whites and Negroes in an urban society makes this possible, even in an era when assumptions about the morality of the pattern of race relations have been dramatically challenged. Recently Louis Lomax wrote of white liberals,

> . . . Few liberals have more than a "headline" acquaintance with the Negro and they join with the general white population in a total ignorance of the Negro's history. And it is for this very reason that even the white liberal is hard pressed to understand the current racial unrest.[4]

## THE SOUTHERN WHITE LIBERAL AS DEVIANT

Within this cultural framework the white liberal who has consciously reached the conclusion that there is a continuing crisis and that the system should change must be regarded as a deviant. He does not accept one important aspect of his familiar culture as natural and right. When he outwardly complies with the prevailing norms, his public compliance is not accompanied by private acceptance. When he refuses to comply with the norms, or challenges them verbally, he marks himself in the eyes of his fellows as a noncomformist. Myrdal's characterization of the southern liberal group is still an apt one:

> It is mostly a fraternity of individuals with independent minds, usually living in, and adjusting to, an uncongenial social surrounding.[5]

Now the nonconformist is not likely to be the person who is near the top of the power structure in his society. It may be that his privately held attitudes, or even his personality, inhibit him from entering a contest for power and success in which he knows that the rules of the game will require him to compromise. Or, if he does enter the contest, his refusal to compromise may limit his attainment of the higher levels of power in a society which mistrusts his deviant ideas. If he is an individual who is able to conceal his deviant attitudes or to gain power in spite of them, he is not likely to express these ideas publicly, even though he may hold them privately. Indeed, it might be postulated that the greater the power and responsibility he acquires, the less likely he is to translate his personal attitudes of noncomformity into public or official action.

The 1958 Report on Race Relations published by Tuskegee Institute characterized the inactivity of influential white citizens and the plight of white liberals in the following contrast:

> Business leaders tended to remain aloof from the controversy and when pressed for opinions usually have not discussed segregation or civil rights. White leaders of the movement for desegregation lacked the rostrum of public office. Their appeals to reason, conscience and civil disobedience have drawn upon them censure, ostracism and persecution from their segregationist opposition.[6]

It must be recognized that most liberals, like most conservatives, cherish many values in addition to those relating to race relations. While there is little that the Negro may do that does not remind him of his status as a Negro, the white man does not most of the time think of himself primarily as a white man. He thinks of himself instead in his other roles as a businessman, a parent, a teacher, a church member, a worker, a politician, or what have you. The Negro lives as an outsider in the white man's world. The white man, even though he may disapprove of it, is an insider in this world. For him to subject it to constant criticism on the basis of the single issue of racial values requires that he jeopardize other values. Hence, the white liberal is handicapped, whether he knows it or not, by a vested interest in the existing order. As Blumer puts it,

> . . . Even though given individual members may have personal views and feelings different from the sense of group position, they will have to conjure with the sense of group position held by their racial group. If the sense of position is strong, to act contrary to it

is to risk a feeling of self-alienation and to face the possibility of ostracism.[7]

There is evidence that many Negroes realize this and lack confidence in the reliability of their liberal white friends in a showdown. Nearly two years ago, Myles Horton, director of the Highlander Folk School, observed that "Negro college students are excluding white youth from inner circles of their demonstration movement" because "they fear the whites may take over the leadership and in some instances don't trust them." [8] In a recent article in *The Reporter,* David Halberstam quotes the Reverend Will Campbell, a self-designated white liberal of the South, as saying that Negroes feel about white liberals now, "You're not prepared to do what needs to be done. You're not prepared to ride buses and sit at counters." Campbell adds, "And of course, in most cases they're right." [9]

## INDIVIDUAL ACTION

What, then, can the white liberal, at war with the normative order of his society and limited in his access to power, do to help bring about the changes he believes are desirable? He could, of course, embark on a quixotic individual campaign, accepting the risk of martyrdom. But he is a member of the mass society in which, as Louis Wirth used to point out, the typical mode of action for the individual is organizational participation. But when the white liberal attempts to act through organizations he is confronted with another dilemma. A logical way for him to exert his influence is through existing associations that have become institutionalized to the extent of being recognized as the legitimate custodians of particular values in the society. These include such organizations as civic clubs, chambers of commerce, labor unions, churches, parent-teacher associations, veterans' organizations, and the like. But almost without exception, these associations have their primary concern with interests and values other than race relations. In spite of its constant and diligent attempts to extend its concern across the whole spectrum of human relations, even the Anti-Defamation League finds that some of its members feel it should be concerned only with the status of the Jewish minority. The difficulties labor unions have experienced in getting their members to accept a generalized concern with the rights of Negroes are well known. If the white liberal attempts to foster an active concern with the problems of Negro–white relations in such organizations, he threatens the values which the more conservative members, and perhaps he himself, regard as paramount. Instead of causing the association to mobilize its resources in support of the values he espouses, he may find himself alienated from his fellow members and regarded as a "crank" or even as a threat. Or, if he gains some support within the organization, he may find that he splits it into factions. The disagreement of these factions over the issue of race relations may make the organization less effective in the promotion of any of its values.

## INTERRACIAL ORGANIZATIONS

In the face of such obstacles to working through established associations, the tendency is for the liberal to seek to form or join new organizations whose primary commitment is to the promotion of racial democracy. The problem of getting agreement on the need for change in the norms of race relations and the status of the Negro is minimized, for members are recruited largely on the basis of their prior commitment to these values. But herein lies the weakness of such organizations. The even more visible activities of a deviant group are substituted for the efforts of the deviant individual. The deviant character of the group is likely to be dramatized by the fact that it is biracial in character, the white liberals being unable to compromise with the central value orientations around which they are united. The fact that the organization begins by openly flouting the norms which it desires to change not only antagonizes people who are firmly committed to the support of these norms but also frightens away conformists who are wavering in their loyalty to the old pattern of race relations. Even though these people might be regarded, in James Russell Lowell's terms, as the cowards who "stand aside till the multitude make virtue of the faith they had denied," they nevertheless may include some of the very people who are in positions to exercise great influence in the community. The result of this process of self-selection is likely to be that the liberal organization commits what Merton has called "the fallacy of group soliloquies." As he put it,

Ethnic liberals are busily engaged in talking to themselves. Repeatedly the same groups of like-minded liberals seek each other out, hold periodic meetings in which they engage in mutual exhortation, and thus lend social and psychological support to one another.[10]

But as George Simpson and Milton Yinger have pointed out,

The all-weather liberal mistakes discussion in like-minded groups for effective action, and overestimates the support for his position.[11]

Having postulated that Merton's characterization of all-weather liberals applies in most cases to the activities of white liberals in the South, let us consider the consequences for the role of the white liberal and liberal organizations vis-à-vis white community leaders and Negro leaders. What often happens, particularly in communities with very conservative leadership, is that the liberal organizations or outspoken liberal individuals come to be regarded either as peculiar or as dangerous. They are not regarded as legitimate forces within the white community but as outsiders who have allied themselves with a threatening Negro movement. Because of this definition of ethnic liberals as marginal to the white community, they may find themselves excluded even from interracial negotiations of an official sort. A liberal group which is biracial in composition may be regarded as even more dangerous and more distasteful than a militant Negro organization because it not only questions the validity of the norms but also violates them.

Finally, the tendency of liberal organizations, firmly committed to the tenets of the American Creed, to operate in an open rather than a subrosa fashion makes them easy targets and readily available scapegoats in periods of racial tension. The white members, particularly if they have children, may be even more vulnerable to informal sanctions than are the Negro members. Their very involvement in white society makes them highly accessible as targets for aggression.

## RELATION TO NEGRO LEADERS

The position of the white liberal in relation to Negro leaders is markedly affected by the situation in which the Negro leader finds himself. At least since the 1954 decisions of the Supreme Court, the Negro leader in the South has found himself operating under a set of pressures very different from those affecting the white liberal. It is quite clearly the conciliatory, accommodating Negro leader, not the militant protest leader, who is the deviant within Negro society today. Whereas white society looks askance at the white liberal who argues for change in the pattern of race relations, Negroes look with deep suspicion on the Negro leader who does not in some way challenge the status quo. In a situation in which change comes slowly and the most dramatic and heroic labors often produce only mouse-like, token results, there is constant pressure for even more militant forms of protest. It is a commonplace observation now among students of race relations that the NAACP has come to be a conservative Negro organization, at least in the eyes of many younger Negroes.

Thus the Negro leader is likely to demand more of white liberals than they are willing to give. The pressures on the white liberal to make haste slowly and to avoid alienating himself from the white ingroup have been enumerated. But if the white liberal responds to these pressures, the Negro is likely to perceive his response as evidence of insincerity or cowardice. At the same time, Negro leaders have an exaggerated notion of the influence their white liberal friends are able to exert. As outsiders to white society, they may forget there is prejudice and discrimination between whites as well as between whites and Negroes. Furthermore, white liberals may contribute to such an unrealistic assessment of their influence by optimistic predictions of the amount of support they might be able to rally. The position of the white liberal in relation to the Negro leader is almost as marginal as is his position in relationship to the influential white leaders. A realistic appraisal of the situation leads to the conclusion that the really dynamic agents in changing patterns of race relations are Negro protest leaders and white defenders of the status quo. The desegregation controversy is not simply a heated debate over abstract principles taking place between the members of a cohesive ingroup. It is battle for status between two hostile interest groups. Changes are most likely to result from a conflict-negotiation-compromise cycle, not from a mass conversion within one of the warring factions.

## THE MARTYR'S ROLE

The white liberal, then, is confronted with a grave dilemma. The dream that he represents a silent South, and that if only he will raise his voice a chorus of the more timorous will join in, is an illusion. If he raises his voice in forceable protest he is more likely to find that his role is that of a voice crying in the wilderness, and he may be cast in the martyr's role.

Such a role may be functional, however. It challenges the complacency of white society by confronting the members, and particularly the leaders, with a moral decision of inescapable gravity. It may also dispel the illusion of unanimity which is a strong support for any dogmatically held position. While the fact that the white liberal is a member of the ingroup may make his nonconformity more infuriating to his fellows, it may also shake their conviction that only "the enemy" disagree with them. But the martyr needs to have a realistic conception of his role. It is unrealistic to expect to be snatched from the flames and elevated to the throne at the last moment. Martyrdom is somewhat different from leadership; the martyr cannot expect to enjoy the fruits of his sacrifice.

## THE "WAITING ROLE"

A less heroic role for the liberal is that of maintaining his solidarity with the white ingroup, challenging the norms subtly and strategically. It involves supporting, rather than threatening, people who are just beginning to question the validity of these norms. Many liberals may, as part of their occupational roles, make small but significant contributions to an intelligent and democratic solution to social problems. Many teachers, ministers, and journalists may be doing just this within whatever degrees of latitude their situations permit. Even this involves risk, for simply asking the wrong questions, or citing unpopular facts, may be defined as dangerous. On the other hand, this role is likely to seem dull, insignificant, and unsatisfying. It accepts gradualism in social change as a premise. It demands rigid self-restraint in the face of the temptation to make the noble gesture and thereby bring about a speedy solution. Yet the oft-repeated observation that the younger generation is more liberal in matters of race relations than the old seems to rest in part on the assumption that such people are having some effect. Perhaps it may be said, in truth, "They also serve who only stand and teach!"

## POTENTIAL ALLIES

In adopting the less dramatic, more unobtrusive role, the liberal may also await the time when more influential members of the white ingroup admit the need for taking action on the problems of race relations. The history of the desegregation controversy shows that they do admit this need when values besides that of segregation are threatened—values such as keeping the schools open, preventing mob violence, and forestalling economic losses. The number of organizations which have arisen to defend such values even at the price of accepting some desegregation far exceeds the number of avowedly "liberal" organizations. It is impossible without further research to say how large a part liberals, as defined here, have played in these organizations. It is quite likely, however, that many of the "silent liberals" have found in them an opportunity to engage in social action supporting peaceful, if gradual, change in patterns of race relations.

Examination of accounts of such organizations as SOS, HOPE, COPE, OASIS, STOP,[12] and others suggests that they share certain important characteristics. One is that they draw widespread support from established associations containing white leaders. These include such groups as chambers of commerce, labor unions, parent-teacher associations, ministerial associations, women's clubs, and business and professional associations. In 1959 the Legal Committee of the Committee for the Peaceful Operation of Our Free Public Schools, in Little Rock, announced that it had 18 lawyers standing by to back the move for court injunctions if needed "to curb agitators." [13]

A second important characteristic is that these organizations attempt to avoid debating the issue of segregation versus integration, appealing instead to other value considerations. Many make it clear that they prefer segregation but are willing to accept some desegregation if it is necessary to preserve other values. One of the most striking instances of a shift of emphasis between competing values was seen in Little Rock in May of 1961. There a group of white parents asked the school board to desegregate an elementary school rather than make it an all-Negro school. Their reason was that it was the only school still open to white children in their part of town. Quite independently, the NAACP was also objecting to the conversion of the school, but on the ground that this would be preserving segregation.[14]

This strange and purely fortuitous alliance points up another feature of the "moderate" organization—willy-nilly its members become allies of the liberals. Whatever their motives, they throw their support on the side of change as against the status quo. Perhaps it is even more significant that, because of the polarization of attitudes that takes place in a community in the midst of controversy, these high-status moderates find themselves subjected to the calumny previously directed at outspoken liberals. In New Orleans, SOS was accused of having some pro-Communists among its leaders.[15] The chairman of HOPE in Atlanta said,

> Georgians who have spoken out for keeping the schools open have exposed themselves to all sorts of abuse and slander.[16]

In such tests of strength in a community, the patient, "moderate" liberal will not find standing up for open schools, or effective law enforcement, safe and easy. He will be called a "scalawag" as surely as if he had chosen to "sit-in" at a lunch counter or join a freedom ride. But he is likely to find that in joining his efforts to those of other moderates, even though they disagree with him on the morality of segregation, he does influence community practices. A minister from Little Rock observed in 1959 that only a few months after Harry Ashmore had concluded that people like himself had "lost at every turn" and were in an untenable position, the city's leading citizens were clamoring for the opening of the schools on a desegregated basis.[17] This minister also observed,

> As a result of their efforts in the STOP movement, the very civic leaders who had refused during the past two years publicly to support Superintendent Blossom's plan of minimum desegregation are now promoting that plan with a crusade-like spirit.[18]

## ALTERNATIVES FOR ACTION

This situational analysis suggests, then, that the white liberal is not likely to exert much influence in the southern community until issues other than segregation versus desegregation arise. He is a deviant in a society in which acceptance of the inferior social position of the Negro is "normal." As a nonconformist, he is not likely to be in, or have access to, the higher levels of the power structure.

So, the white liberal may attempt to precipitate a crisis by playing the martyr, thereby bringing such values as fair play and justice into focus. He may, on the other hand, accept the less heroic role of the moderate until a community crisis presents him with the opportunity to ally himself with other, more conservative but more influential moderates. But for him to enjoy the satisfaction of becoming the self-anointed leader of a popular crusade for changes in the pattern of race relations is not a live option.

## NOTES

1. Myrdal, *op. cit.*, p. 470.
2. Governor Ross Barnett, quoted in *Southern School News,* October, 1959, p. 3.
3. Herbert Blumer, "Race Prejudice as a Sense of Group Position," *Pacific Sociological Review,* I (Spring, 1958), p. 4.
4. Louis Lomax, *op. cit.,* p. 5.
5. Myrdal, *op. cit.,* p. 467.
6. Quoted in *Southern School News,* February, 1959, p. 16.
7. Blumer, *op. cit.,* p. 5.
8. Quoted in *Southern School News,* May, 1960, p. 6.
9. David Halberstam, "The Kids Take Over," *The Reporter,* June 22, 1961, pp. 22-23.
10. Robert K. Merton, in R. M. MacIver (ed.), *Discrimination and National Welfare,* Institute for Religious and Social Studies (distributed by Harper & Row, Publishers), 1949, p. 104.
11. George E. Simpson and Milton Yinger, *Racial and Cultural Minorities,* rev. ed. (New York: Harper & Row, Publishers, 1958), p. 728.
12. SOS—Save Our Schools, Inc. (New Orleans); COPE—Committee On Public Education (New Orleans); HOPE—Help Our Public Education (Atlanta); OASIS—Organizations Assisting Schools in September (Atlanta); STOP—Committee to Stop This Outrageous Purge (Arkansas).

13. *Southern School News,* September, 1959, p. 2.
14. *Southern School News,* June, 1961, p. 13.
15. *Southern School News,* January, 1961, p. 10.
16. *Southern School News,* March, 1960, p. 15.
17. Colbert S. Cartwright, "Hope Comes to Little Rock," *The Progressive,* August, 1959, pp. 7-9.
18. *Ibid.*

# SIX

# Tokenism—
# Too Little, Too Late

If "better race relations" signifies the achievement of fuller participation in American society by the Negro along with the reduction of intergroup conflict, then the picture presented here is a dark one. The biracial "team" approach produces only a superficial type of communication. The changes this approach is likely to produce are insignificant in comparison with the results of independent, aggressive action by militant Negro leaders who approach the white power structure with threats, not petitions. But even the new, "protest" leaders, with their militant tactics, often win only token victories. Their plight is like that of a man trying to put out a bonfire with a teacup. As each ember is extinguished through "tokenism," the fire blazes more furiously in another place and demands more heroic efforts to smother the glowing core of discontent. The white liberal can give moral support to the Negro, but he has not proven to be a principal combatant in this power struggle. There is, moreover, growing evidence that important Negro leaders are losing faith in his value to them.

But perhaps this is a time to be pessimistic. Through pessimism we may come closer to a realistic appraisal of the persistent problem of Negro–white relations, a problem which may be no closer to a solution now than it was a century ago. To suggest that so little progress has been made toward reconciling the realities of race relations with the ideals of the American Creed is to defy the "pervasive strain of optimism, belief in progress, and faith in the perfectibility of human society which have deep roots in American culture." [1] This belief in progress leads to the assumption that there must surely have been progress in race relations. Has not the Negro been freed from slavery and made a citizen? Have not lynchings been virtually abolished? Has not segregation been declared unconstitutional? Are not the walls of segregation indeed crumbling? Is not a younger generation of white Americans, together with many of their elders, accepting the idea that integration is inevitable? Do not many white citizens, even those who vigorously oppose every step toward integration, privately admit, "It's coming"?

The vague notion of "the inevitability of integration" is one of the clearest illustrations of the strain of optimism. As used by most white people, it represents a peculiar, nonrevolutionary type of optimism (or, in the case of the segregationist, of resignation). Its coming to pass is not even related to an approximate time in the future, but to a time that is always over the horizon. More important, achievement of this solution is related to no critical event nor to the climax of a series of events. There seems to be the assumption that gradually, almost painlessly, the present alienation of the Negro community from American society will be eroded away until assimilation takes place.

Under this assumption, the pace of the "progress" which has already taken place will gradually be speeded up and resistance will become steadily weaker. The integrative effects of consensus about the American Creed, as well as the cohesive qualities of the American social system, will limit the destructiveness of the explosion triggered by the collision of white and Negro interests. True, some conflict is contemplated in this optimistic model. But conflict is viewed as episodic, incidental, and, despite all contradictions, "innoculative." On all sides there is a tremendous confidence that each episode of violence will, like an antitoxin, reduce the likelihood of a recurrence. Yet Oxford followed Little Rock, and Alabama derived no immunity to conflict from the blood bath of neighboring Mississippi!

Questioning this blind, optimistic faith in the inevitability of integration does not require adoption of the equally naïve "optimism" (from their point of view) of the die-hard segregationists. They dream of the restoration of a condition which, if it ever existed at all, is truly "gone with the wind." The optimistic segregationist is as unwilling as the optimistic integrationist to face realistically the inevitability of conflict as a social process. He dreams of a system of segregation and white supremacy maintained not through power and conflict but through the gracious paternalism of whites and the happy subservience of Negroes. The myth of "the happy Negro" which persisted simply because the balance of power was so one-sided has been dispelled by the reality of growing Negro power.

The fact that the segregation characteristic of the era of accommodation is finished does not mean, however, that progressive, essentially peaceful integration is inevitable. The Negro is still faced with his ancient problem, the problem of being a black man in America, a white man's world. Here there is a rarely noticed identity between the premises of both white segregationists and white integrationists. The segregationist recognizes that it is a white man's world and frankly proposes to bar the Negro's entrance into it. The integrationist invites the Negro to enter it but assumes that it will remain the same white man's world. The segregationist expresses fear of Negro political domination if Negroes obtain the vote in "Black Belt" counties. The integrationist replies that Negroes vote in blocs only when race is an issue, implying that a white numerical minority would still have proportional or even preeminent influence in local government. The segregationist protests that desegregation of schools will lower the educational and moral standards of the white children. The integrationist explains that, in the *white* schools, the Negroes will be "brought up" to white standards. (That there might be anything for the white children to gain in this acculturation process is rarely suggested.) When the segregationist raises the question of intermarriage, the integrationist objects that the question is irrelevant, a diversionary tactic, and that Negroes are not really interested in intermarriage. Nowhere does one find the suggestion that making the Negro a full partner in American life might entail the development of the Brazilian attitude toward amalgamation—acceptance of the process as "a matter of course and, to a certain extent, a point of pride." [2]

This possibility is an embarrassing secret which is rarely brought into the light except by the segregationist. If the advocate of equality for the Negro does mention it, he is likely to dismiss it as a remote eventuality which the white man must "risk" if he is to correct present injustices. The remoteness of this risk to white "purity" is suggested in the words of Lillian Smith,

> Old prejudices will linger in many minds a long time after legal segregation disappears. Social barriers will crumble slowly. But here and there a young woman, a young man, will choose to marry into the other group. [3]

The sociological arguments in support of this proposition are abundant. But the question remains. What happens while this long, tortuous process is going on? Will not the large majority of Negroes still remain an unassimilated minority in an essentially white America? Will they not still be desperately seeking an identity of which they can be proud? And will the Negro who seems to have been accepted in the white world have truly found such an identity? Will he not be, instead, a marginal man who really belongs in the still extant Negro world notwithstanding his acceptance on sufferance in a white world that regards him as an exception and tries to overlook his Negro ancestry?

In short, will ever-so-gradual "token integration," even with "token amalgamation," really lead to the solution of the Negro's problem of status and identity? At the present time, integration as a solution to the race problem demands that the Negro foreswear his identity as a Negro. But for a lasting solution, the meaning of "American" must lose its implicit racial modifier, "white." Even without biological amalgamation, integration requires a sincere acceptance by all Americans that it is just as good to be a black American as to be a white American. Here is the crux of the problem of race relations—the redefinition of the sense of group position so that the status advantage of the white man is no longer an advantage, so that an American may acknowledge his Negro ancestry without apologizing for it.

It is the progress that may have been made toward the solution of this problem that is questioned here. It is easy to measure progress objectively if an arbitrary criterion is selected and the subjective reactions of the human actors are disregarded. To a historian, a state of freedom may signify the progress of a people who were once in slavery. But to the individual who is born into freedom and yet finds that he cannot be fully a man, it is no consolation to know that had he been born a century earlier, he would have been a slave. He measures progress not historically and objectively, but subjectively in terms of his own aspirations and the prospects of achieving them. He has no "racial memory" of the sufferings of his ancestors under slavery, but he has a clear consciousness of present frustrations and indignities. And in the affluence of twentieth-century America, the Negro people are still desperately far from achieving material equality. Worse, they are far from achieving a satisfying identity either as

Americans or as Negroes. They live in a society in which to be un-conditionally "American" is to be white, and to be black is a misfor-tune. As Essien-Udom expresses it,

> A century after the Emancipation, nineteen million black Ameri-cans, robbed of their traditions and of a pride in their past, are still seeking acceptance by the white majority but are continuing to live in semibondage on the fringes of American society.[4]

This semibondage is not only economic but is also psychological, for the Negro American can neither forget that he is black nor be proud of it. The question that presses for an answer today is whether Negroes in America will wait patiently while the slow, peaceful, democratic process of integration evolves. There is little evidence that white society will be willing to give up its sense of dominance without a struggle. Nor is there much evidence that white Americans are willing to make sufficient sacrifices to speed up the process of inte-gration and overtake the increasing alienation of the masses of Negro Americans.

Perhaps a foundation could have been laid for the peaceful, pro-gressive integration of Negroes into American society during the period of Reconstruction, with its forgotten alternatives. The pleas of George Washington Cable, voiced in the waning days of the nine-teenth century, bear eloquent testimony to the opportunities that existed for the Negro to come up from slavery as the southern white man came up from defeat. Almost a century later the painstaking historical research of C. Vann Woodward establishes the fact that a different road was open to the South from the one it took. But the white South of that day, with the acquiescence and even the col-laboration of the white North, chose to postpone the granting of equal opportunity and equal dignity to the Negro. Looking back to another crossroads in American history, Cable prophesied fruitlessly but ac-curately. He spoke of the time of the founding of the nation:

> . . . Our fathers were bitten with the delusion of postponement and the practice of slavery became an Institution. . . . The problem before us is the green, rank stump of that felled Institution. Slavery in particular—the slavery of the individual man to his one master, which rested upon the law, is by the law abolished. Slavery in gen-eral—the subordination of a fixed rule to a fixed ruling class—the

slavery of civil caste, which can only in part, and largely cannot, be legislated away, remains. Sad will it be if we leave it for their inheritance.[5]

Whatever might have been, this inheritance was left not only to the South but to the entire nation. Legal and social segregation developed to mold the pattern of race relations in the South. As thousands of Negro peasants flowed into northern, and later, western cities, ecological segregation became the matrix for the development of racial inequality outside the South. Now, with the urbanization of the South, the urban Negro ghetto has assumed its place as the modern counterpart of the plantation as the physical basis for race relations.[6]

Three quarters of a century after the United States Supreme Court struck down the civil rights laws of 1875 which might have forestalled the development of segregation as an institution, the Court overthrew its own legal fiction of "separate but equal," which in effect sanctioned the development of segregation and inequality. But events of the decade which has passed since the school decision of 1954 testify to the truth of Cable's prediction that "the slavery of civil caste can only in part be legislated away." During the more than half-century in which Negroes have been excluded from full participation in American life, the barriers to assimilation have become stronger and more complex. There are four of these barriers. They are:

1. The entrenchment of the white man's sense of group position not only in the South, but throughout the nation.
2. The continuing spatial segregation of Negroes.
3. The cultural deficit of the Negro masses in a rapidly changing culture.
4. The enduring reality of the Negro community.

## THE WHITE MAN'S SENSE OF GROUP POSITION

Prejudice against Negroes may have become more entrenched over the years. To say this is to fly in the face of many attitude studies and impressionistic observations. There seems to have been a statistical shift in the distribution of attitudes about why the Negro is inferior, what constitutes acceptable behavior toward individual Negroes, and the inconsistency of gross discrimination with the American Creed. But prejudice assumes many forms, and what we are seeing may simply be a shift to subtler, more genteel forms. The essential sociological question is whether the collective sense of group position on which the American social order has been historically based has changed significantly. Herbert Blumer has observed,

> Race prejudice becomes entrenched and tenacious to the extent the prevailing social order is rooted in the sense of social position. This has been true of the historic South in our country. In such a social order race prejudice tends to become chronic and impermeable to change.[7]

But growing resistance to *de facto* desegregation in housing, schools, and employment in New York, Chicago, Philadelphia, Los Angeles, Berkeley and other nonsouthern cities, makes it increasingly evident that the South has no monopoly on the spirit of white supremacy. The feeling that the superior white race, with its propriety claim to certain areas of privilege and advantage, is being threatened by an intrinsically different, alien, and subordinate group, is national, not just southern. Partly through the unplanned, ecological patterns of urban growth, partly because of the impersonality of urban life, nonsouthern whites have been able to retreat into their all-white suburbs and private clubs and thereby maintain the pretense that they are different from southern segregationists. But with the continued migration of Negroes from the South, the reluctance of large numbers of white Americans, in no matter what region, to accept the Negro as a neighbor, not just a "problem" or a "cause," has become painfully evident. And the token integration of a few Negroes into what remain essentially white businesses, colleges, hotels, and churches does not counterbalance the continued massing of Negroes in the black ghettoes and the inexorable flow of these ghettoes to engulf transitional areas, often to the accompaniment of bombs, screaming mobs, and police sirens!

Furthermore, when sociologists have taken the trouble to study the place of the Negro in smaller cities and towns in the North, not in the densely populated urban "jungles," they have found the white man's sense of group position to be just as strong as it is in the South, although more subtly manifested. In an upstate New York community of 60,000 persons, Robert Johnson found,

When the majority group was asked about the Negro community, it soon became evident that most majority group members had (a) very little contact with Negroes, and (b) a great deal of prejudice against them.[8]

That this "statistical picture of anti-Negro prejudice" was a manifestation of an entrenched status system was shown by the finding that white respondents consistently imputed to other white people even more conservative attitudes than they themselves expressed. Johnson concluded that the pattern of subtle prejudice and discrimination confronted the Negro with a barrier which produced in him a pattern of avoidance and defensive insulation.

Frank F. Lee found similar conditions in an even smaller town in New England, selected because just such an area "is usually thought to be 'liberal' in terms of race relations."[9] With only 170 Negroes in a population of 10,000, the town has a clearly recognized "Negro section" and Negroes are concentrated almost exclusively in the lower levels of employment. Although Lee found more deviations from the pattern than would be expected in a southern town, he described the general pattern in these terms:

> Nevertheless discrimination and segregation do exist, and while the outlines of the pattern may be vague, the core of it is solid. Some statuses which are open to whites are closed to Negroes, and while Negroes may be admitted to others, they are not allowed full participation. The Negro therefore lives in a somewhat separate world: he inhabits certain sections of town; he has his own church and social activities; and he is barred from most of the private clubs and organizations and from many public facilities.[10]

Of the exceptional Negroes who were able to break through the wall of the separate world, he observed:

> Such a Negro tends to serve as a positive contrast to the mass of Negroes and to be considered "different." Thus, paradoxically, he demonstrates the continued vigor of the traditional status definition, even while he suggests that this definition lacks the full force of the mores, and may, as conditions alter, be susceptible to change.[11]

These two studies of race relations in communities with very small Negro populations, lacking "southern traditions," and located in states which have civil rights laws and commissions, demonstrate the pervasiveness of the sense of "the Negro's place" as an alien and a social inferior throughout American society. Summing up studies of the Negro's position based on "social-distance scales," Muzafer and Carolyn Sherif observe that there is a scale of social distances established throughout the United States, accepted in some degree by the overwhelming majority of people, and remaining remarkably consistent over a long time period.[12] The Negro remains near the bottom of this scale, below even recent immigrant groups. Members of America's newest minority, the Puerto Ricans, have found that it is still better to be an unacculturated "Latin" than an acculturated "Negro."

From 1875 until 1954, the government of the United States, through adherence to the fiction of "separate but equal," gave indirect sanction and even encouragement to this definition of the Negro's place. The school desegregation decision of the Supreme Court did not really change this pattern of exclusion. It simply withdrew the federal sanction for the pattern and gave Negroes a new legal weapon. But the conservative white power elite still possessed many weapons for resisting any fundamental change in the Negro's status. As Woodward said,

> The reformers were . . . divided in council, restrained by constitutional scruples, and reluctant, most of them, to resort to coercion and force.[13]

Commenting on the way Americans typically respond to reformers, he noted:

> It is true that the present Court has consistently held against segregation. But Americans have developed over the years a curious usage of the laws as an appeasement of moralists and reformers. Given sufficient pressure for a law that embodies reputable and popular moral values, the electorate will go to great lengths to gratify the reformers. . . . But having done this much, they are inclined to regard it as rather tedious of the reformers to insist upon literal enforcement. Under these circumstances the new law is likely to become the subject of pious reference, more honored in the breach than in the observance, a proof of excellent intentions rather than the means of fulfilling them.[14]

"Tokenism" represents just such an adjustment. Max Ascoli, editor of *The Reporter,* has characterized tokenism as "symbolic com-

pliance made persuasive with a minimum of physical reality." [15]
Recognition of this fact by militant Negro leaders triggered the
"Negro Revolt" beginning in 1959. What appears as softening of resistance to desegregation in the South may merely be expediency.
It reflects a recognition by the forces of resistance that it is easier
and cheaper to comply symbolically by accepting a few "exceptional"
Negroes in white institutions than it is to resist symbolically by fighting federal pressure to the bitter end. Of greater significance is the
fact that this sort of symbolic compliance is so often acclaimed as
"progress" by white liberals, apparently on the assumption that the
admission of the first Negro will, as the segregationists gloomily
predict, lead inexorably to the breaking down of all barriers against
all Negroes. There is a reluctance to face the possibility that it might
lead only to the subtle pattern of exclusion and dominance described
by Johnson and Lee, with a small number of "integrated" Negroes
representing exceptions to the pattern. They would still be refugees
from an inferior, unassimilated Negro community. That this is a real
possibility is indicated by the spatial segregation and the cultural
deprivation which make the road of tokenism impossible for the large
majority of Negro Americans.

## NEW PATTERNS OF SEGREGATION

One of the salient factors influencing the destiny of Negroes in
the United States was their concentration, for so much of their
history, in the rural areas of the South. The far-reaching effects of
this pattern of distribution on the social and economic system of the
South, on the Negro's mode of life in that region, and on his subsequent adjustment to life in other regions have been well-documented.
But the decade of 1950-1960 marks the end of this historic pattern
and the clear emergence of new patterns of segregation. In 1910 some
89.0 percent of the Negroes in the United States lived in the South,
and as late as 1950, 68.0 percent lived there, but by 1960 just slightly
over one half remained in the region. [16] In 1910 just a little over one
quarter of the Negroes lived in urban areas, but by 1950 two thirds
were urban dwellers, and by 1960 almost three quarters lived in
cities, large or small. Outside the South, Negroes have always been
primarily urban residents, but by 1960 nearly 60 percent of the
Negroes living in the South were classified as urban. This signifies a

major change in the background of race relations. From being a predominantly southern and rural population, the Negro minority has become a national and urban community. But there is no assurance that this redistribution will ameliorate the Negro's problems. It may, instead, exacerbate them. This is not a process of dispersion and spatial desegregation. It is, rather, a process of relocation and "re-segregation."

Washington typifies this new pattern of Negro living. Negroes in the District of Columbia, the central city, have increased more rapidly than whites and now constitute 54 percent of the city's population. The nation's capital is a dramatic symbol of a widespread trend. In the decade between 1950 and 1960 the proportion of non-whites in the central city increased in all of the fifty largest cities in the United States, North, South, East and West. Within its city limits, New York had over a million Negroes; Chicago, 890,000; Los Angeles, 334,000; Houston, 215,000; and Atlanta, 186,000.[17]

Such aggregations of Negroes represent segregation on a grand scale; the urban "black belts" dwarf the old "colored sections" of small southern towns. As sociologists Leo Schnore and Harry Sharp have commented, metropolitan "rings"—the suburbs outside the central cities—are overwhelmingly white, and there is evidence that the proportion of nonwhites is declining in many suburban rings, particularly in the South.[18] Experiments in integrated housing (almost exclusively in the North) and governmental lip-service to "open occupancy standards," whether in private or public housing, have been ineffective in stemming this tide. Frank S. Horne, of the New York Mayor's Commission on Intergroup Relations, states the case bluntly:

> The harsh reality is that the seemingly relentless ghetto trend takes place under a smoke screen created by the very "gains" so welcomed by proponents of civil rights. This trend moves on—while we hail the enactment or introduction of anti-discrimination laws in state and municipal legislatures throughout the North and West and while we hopefully survey experience with "open occupancy" developments.[19]

Even in those northern and western cities where city planners and other officials strive to develop neighborhoods that are both "mixed" and stable, the task of dispersing hundreds of thousands of Negroes from black ghettoes is formidable. Negroes moved from the ghettoes are more than replaced by the constant stream of migrants from rural areas. The movement of farm population, particularly Negroes, to the cities exceeds that of any other migratory period in United States history. In the South, efforts to deal with the problems this creates have hardly even begun, for the problem of the urban Negro ghetto is just beginning to be recognized there. In cities, both South and North, this is a problem which is steadily growing worse. As James Conant has forcefully declared, "We are allowing social dynamite to accumulate in our large cities." [20]

The level of living and the cultural standards of the masses of Negroes trapped in these densely populated, continuously deteriorating ghettoes are not likely to keep pace with "the American way of life." Hence there is great danger that, for countless Negroes, faith in America will be drowned in this black sea. Their isolation from white Americans will be magnified and, in their bitterness and isolation, they may be mobilized for violent conflict against people who need only to be recognized as white to be identified as enemies.

Perhaps the plight of the Negro in the urban slum is no worse than that of his fellow in small southern towns. The still pervasive surveillance of the small-town southern white society smothers the slightest stir of protest. But it is in the cities that most Negro Americans now live. In the cities the dynamite is waiting for the spark, and there is the hard core of "the Negro problem."

## LAST MAN ON THE ESCALATOR

One of the sources of the pride, the optimism and, at times the complacency, of the American people today is the ever rising level of living. This level is usually measured by such criteria as higher income, better housing, more automobiles, TV sets and bathtubs, and greater average educational attainments. It is easy to show that the American people have achieved "the highest standard of living in the world" and that even Negro Americans live better, on the average than all the people of many nations. But Negro Americans are not living in these other nations; they are living in twentieth-century America, measuring their level of living by American standards. The American people are, as it were, standing on an escalator moving upward toward a level which must be there, but which can't be seen. The Negro, however, is in the position of the man who stepped on the escalator late. Even though he, too, may move upward, and may even gain a few steps on his fellow passengers, he is still the last man on the escalator! Perhaps he might catch up if he ran, but he is restrained from running by the weight of burdens he carries and by signs on all sides that say "Don't Run!"

Comparison of the income of white and nonwhite Americans (to all effects and purposes, Negro Americans) since mid-century shows how slowly and unsurely the Negro approaches the white man.[21] In 1954, the year the Supreme Court forced Americans to look inequality squarely in the face, the median annual income of white families was $4,339; of nonwhite families, $2,410. The nonwhite median income was 56 percent that of the white. Three years later, in 1957, the white income had increased by 10.1 percent to $5,166, but the Negro had slipped back. Nonwhite income had increased only 14.7 percent to $2,764 a year, and was now only 53.5 percent of the white income. In another three years the Negro had almost regained the loss, for median family income had increased by 17 percent while the white income had increased only 13 percent. The uncertain and tantalizing course of change continued between 1960 and 1961, when the median family income of nonwhites actually decreased by 1.3 percent, while that of white families was increasing by 2.5 per cent. So, the Negro had lost ground again—his income was now only 53.4 percent that of the white American, a net loss of 2.6 percentage points since 1954!

The long-term trend in Negro income since the turn of the century has been to close the gap between it and white income. Recent changes may represent only a temporary recession in the Negro's fortunes. But there is a grim possibility that these changes mark the reversal of the trend—the gap may continue to widen. In the latter half of the twentieth century a new pattern of occupational distribution has emerged, a pattern which gives the concept "technological unemployment" added significance. Charles E. Silberman characterizes this trend:

> The Europeans immigrated during periods of rapidly expanding U.S. demand for unskilled labor; no great transfer of skill was needed to enable an Irish or Italian peasant to find a job on a con-

struction gang. But in the U.S. today, the demand for unskilled labor is shrinking relative to the total labor force. Since 1947, employment of white-collar workers—executives, entrepreneurs, professional and scientific employees, clerks, and salesmen—has gone up 43 percent compared to only a 14 percent gain in blue-collar and service-work employment. By 1970 a substantial majority of workers will be in white-collar or highly skilled blue-collar jobs—in jobs that require real training and thought.[22]

The nation is now faced with a problem of "hard-core" unemployment of older workers who have lost their jobs or younger people who have never had a job, people who are unskilled, untrained, and therefore unemployable in a "skilled society." Negroes, and particularly Negro youth, are disproportionately represented in this hard core. James Conant dramatized this problem in his book, *Slums and Suburbs:*

> In a slum section composed almost entirely of Negroes in one of our largest cities, the following situation was found: A total of 59 percent of the male youth between the ages of 16 and 21 were out of school and unemployed. They were roaming the streets. Of the boys who graduated from high school, 48 percent were unemployed in contrast to 63 percent of the boys who had dropped out of school. In short, about two thirds of the male dropouts did not have jobs and about half of the high school graduates did not have jobs.[23]

For many Americans this is an era of prosperity, but for a large percentage of Negroes entering the labor market it is a time of economic hardship like the great depression. Many young Negroes have already fallen into the abyss of unemployment, and even Negroes who are supposedly secure in their unskilled and semiskilled jobs may be closer to the brink than they or anyone else realizes. An omen of the precariousness of their position is seen in how the influx of Cuban refugees affected the workers of Miami. Testifying at a congressional hearing, a Negro grocer, one of several witnesses, said:

> There is more hunger in Miami's colored districts than there was during the great depression, and robbery is on the increase because most of the workers displaced by Cubans have been Negroes.[24]

This witness went on to observe that "bringing specialized industries into the area to provide employment would not help the Negro because he cannot handle the skilled work." He said, "all the Negroes want are jobs as hotel help and domestics they had before the Cuban influx." [25]

Statistics are cited optimistically to show that the Negro has gained a toe hold in the higher levels of employment. But they do not warrant the assumption that the rule "last hired, first fired" has really changed, particularly for the large number of Negroes still concentrated in the lower levels of skill.

The prejudice of white employers is only one factor explaining the Negro's employment situation. Another factor is that, as "last man on the escalator," the Negro worker is likely to have little seniority in newly opened areas of employment. Moreover, the Negro segment of the labor force still lacks the whole-hearted support of organized labor. But the most significant fact about the employment status of the Negro is his continued concentration in the low-skill occupations in an economy which has less and less requirement for unskilled workers. It is true that there has been a small but steady increase in the proportion of Negroes in white-collar occupations—professional, managerial, clerical and sales work. But the census data do not reveal to what extent this gain may have resulted from the creation of more *segregated* jobs in the "service structure" of burgeoning urban, Negro communities. Moreover, in May, 1962, only 24 percent of nonwhite workers in the U.S. held "high level" jobs (professional, managerial, clerical, sales, craftsmen and foremen) as compared to 61 percent of white workers.[26] At the other end of the occupational ladder, 38.7 of nonwhite workers had employment as domestic servants, in other service jobs, and as laborers, as compared to only 12.2 percent of white workers. This relative distribution has changed very little since 1940, when 35.9 percent of the nonwhite male workers and 13 percent of white male workers were in the low-skill occupations. Another 22.5 percent of Negro male workers were employed as operatives. This seems to represent a great gain since 1940, when only 12.4 percent worked as operatives. But it should be remembered that these workers are in semiskilled jobs where job security is precarious in the absence of seniority and where the threat of automation is the greatest.

There is no clear-cut evidence that the Negro is moving inexorably toward a position of equality in the American economy; there are signs that he may be slipping back slowly. Unless future generations of Negro youth are enabled, and motivated, to acquire the skills demanded by an industrial society, the Negro may slip back even more rapidly in the future. It is these factors that have caused Daniel Bell to predict,

> If we correlate, roughly, the school dropout rate with the skill requirements of the future labor force, then we can say—admittedly a vast simplification and perhaps overly dramatized in order to highlight the case—that 30 years hence, class society in the U.S. will be predominantly color society.[27]

Every serious student of the problems of unemployment and underemployment suggests that, to an increasing degree, occupational status in America is tied to educational achievement. And, despite token integration and expanded expenditures on Negro schools, the Negro continues to lag dangerously in educational preparation for the type of society he is entering. Most dismal is the plight of the "dropout to nowhere," the youth who enters the labor market without having finished high school. According to Naomi Barko,

> The National Committee on Employment of Youth . . . estimates that in Negro slum neighborhoods, youth unemployment runs as high as 35 to 40 percent, with a 50-percent rate for dropouts.[28]

There are superficial indications that Negroes are making slow but steady progress toward closing the educational gap. In 1940 only 3.8 percent of nonwhite males in the U.S. were high school graduates as compared to 12.8 percent of white males. By 1950 these percentages had risen to 7.2 percent for nonwhites and 18.7 percent for whites. In 1960, 12.1 percent of nonwhites and 22.2 percent of white males were high school graduates. Some 10.3 percent of the whites had completed college as compared to 3.5 percent of the nonwhites.

This does not prove, however, that the lag in the educational preparation, even of those Negroes who stay in school, is being closed significantly. The great majority of Negroes, North and South, still attend what are, in fact, "Negro schools." That the quality of the education which they receive in these schools is inferior to that provided in the white schools is well-established. Eli Ginsberg reports the results of a special study conducted in 81 segregated high schools in the large cities in the South in 1953-1954.[29] The conclusion reached was that "only three out of every hundred graduates from segregated Negro high schools in the South were qualified for a good interracial college on the basis of a modified college entrance examination." It is little wonder that Ginsberg reached the pessimistic conclusion—

> If the color barrier could be eliminated overnight, that fact alone would not materially improve the [occupational] position of the Negro. Just as white men now must compete with each other in terms of aptitude, education, and skill, so too does this same challenge face the Negro as the artificial employment barriers which stand in his way are successively eliminated.[30]

The educational achievement of Negroes in the state of Florida, often regarded as one of the most progressive of southern states and most moderate in the area of race relations, provides a good illustration of the plight of the Negro in a rapidly changing, skill-oriented society. When the U.S. Supreme Court knocked out the legal foundation of school segregation laws in 1954, the admission criterion for the state universities was graduation from an accredited high school. Of course, the state's segregation laws dictated that those Negroes who did attend college would be admitted to Florida A. & M. University for Negroes. Theoretically, however, abrogation of the segregation laws would mean that the great majority of the Negro high school graduates would be eligible for admission to the two white universities in the state.

Although, legally eligible, most Negroes were not academically qualified for admission. The results of various standardized tests showed this, particularly the "Florida Twelfth Grade Test," given to all high school seniors since 1949. In 1954, some 93.6 percent of the Negro seniors who took this test scored lower than 50 percent of the white seniors.[31] A score of 200 represented the point below which approximately 40 percent of the white students fell. Of the Negro students, 90 percent made scores lower than 200. This test does not purport to be an "intelligence test"; it is designed to test achievement in the fields of English, mathematics, science, social studies and humanities. Experience over the years had shown that white students who entered the state universities with scores of less than 200 had no better than a 50-50 chance of performing satisfactorily in college.

Even if Florida opened wide the doors of the white universities most Negro high school graduates would find themselves in a hopelessly frustrating situation.

But before any of these Negroes had an opportunity to try to swim in such deep water, far-reaching changes in the philosophy of higher education took place in Florida as in the entire nation. Partly in response to political forces seeking a way to cushion the impact of the desegregation decision, partly as a result of a long-standing desire of many faculty members to raise standards and exclude poorly prepared students, the score on the Twelfth Grade Test was made *part* of the admission requirements in 1957. The growing problem of an increasing demand for space in the already overcrowded universities, the shock of learning that the Russians had been able to launch their "sputnik" ahead of our first earth satellite, and the demands of such spokesmen as Admiral Hyman Rickover for "quality education" in American schools combined to generate increasingly rigorous admission policies—so-called "selective admission." In 1957 a test score of 200 was established as the "automatic cut-off point." If a high school graduate scored this high, he would be admitted to the state universities without special consideration. By 1962, the great majority of the freshmen entering the white universities had scores of 300 or above.

Obviously many white youth found it harder to get into college than it would have been ten years earlier. But for the vast majority of Negro youth in the state, this philosophy of "quality education" had rendered the principle of desegregation virtually meaningless! Of 6,673 Negro high school seniors who took the Twelfth Grade Test in the spring of 1962, only 139, or 2 percent, made scores of 300 or better on the test! Only 475, slightly over 7 percent, scored 200 or higher. In the same year, 41 percent of white high school seniors scored 300 or better, and 64 percent scored 200 or better. But 93 percent of the Negro seniors scored less than 200, an even higher proportion than the 90 percent in 1954!

These data show how little meaning the desegregation of white colleges has for most Negroes. The data also pose serious questions as to the quality of education for Negroes at all levels, including the predominantly Negro colleges in which the vast majority of Negro school teachers are trained. In Florida, for example, the still segregated Negro university must draw most of its students from the more than 90 percent of Negro high school graduates who do not meet the very minimum standards for entering the theoretically de-segregated colleges. The automatic cut-off score for Florida A. & M. University is 200, but all the universities are permitted to admit "unqualified" students on the recommendation of a faculty com-mittee which considers other factors, such as standing in class and grade-point average. But the fact remains that, no matter how well qualified he himself must be, the Negro college professor must work with material that is substandard. It is doubtful that academic standards can or will be raised in the Negro colleges as they are being raised in the white colleges. Nor will the draining off of the exceptional, "qualified" Negro students by their token integra-tion into the white colleges help to improve the academic atmosphere in which the majority of Negro college students seem destined to be trained under present conditions. Even worse, there is every reason to believe that the system of education for Negroes, predominantly seg-regated *de facto,* if not by design, constitutes a vicious circle in which educational inferiority perpetuates itself. Undereducated parents send culturally deprived children to school to be taught by inadequately prepared teachers and to go, in turn, to inferior Negro colleges to become the parents and teachers of yet another generation of Negro children!

The cheapest and most comfortable response for white Ameri-cans to make to this dilemma is to assert, "This simply shows that Negroes are indeed inferior in learning capacity; therefore, nothing can be done about it." This argument is being revived in many quar-ters in spite of evidence accumulated, during nearly half a century, to show its speciousness: Not enough of the variables which influence scores on standardized tests have been controlled or even identified to justify inferences about the distribution of innate ability in differ-ent human groups. The question of whether continued substandard achievement levels by Negro students is to be explained by racial ability or by cultural deprivation cannot be answered now, if ever, but this does not change the essential nature of the problem. This is the fact that, as the economy has less and less use for the unskilled laborer, black or white, the white dominant group must pay the price of continued Negro inequality in one way or another.

The price may be ever-expanding funds for public relief pro-grams. On the other hand, the price may be intensified conflict with a

Negro community that seeks a solution on its own terms. It is well to remember that the dynamic Malcolm X, one of the newest stars in Negro leadership, was a "dropout" from the eighth grade, a juvenile delinquent, and a convict before he climbed to the position of second in command of the Black Muslims!

## THE ENDURING NEGRO COMMUNITY

Excluded or cast out of the community, the lone individual either perishes or becomes an antisocial hermit, an eccentric or a rogue. But when the excluded human being has company in his exile, he and his fellow outsiders form a new community. If this community is accepted as an unequal segment of the larger social system from which the members are partially excluded, it constitutes a minority community.

Newcomers to the United States, lacking the cultural qualifications for immediate assimilation into American society, have formed immigrant communities. The "Little Italys" and the "Chinatowns" of American cities have served as both "a home away from home" for the immigrant and a way station on his road to acculturation and assimilation. Once the minority community has emerged as a viable social entity, it can be as much a trap as it is a way station. In it the individual member of the minority group can find security and acceptance which he risks if he pioneers in the larger community. He can compete more confidently, for in the larger society he would be judged by the standards of a group which has played the game longer than he has. By the same token, he can achieve prestige which comes more easily because the competition is restricted. The restrictions developed by the dominant group to repel the upward mobile minority-group member set up, by a sort of induction, forces in the minority community which must also be overcome if he is to escape.

For over two hundred years the Negro American has not been a stranger in the land. He has nonetheless found himself isolated, ecologically and socially, in the land of his birth. Whether on the plantations of the Old South, in the Smoky Hollows of southern towns, or in the Black Belts of the cities, Negroes have created and sustained Negro communities which are enduring, not evanescent, realities. In them Negroes have for years lived a large part, and certainly the most vibrant, authentic part, of their lives. Perhaps the Negro community has been, as Myrdal suggested, "a pathological form of an American community," but it has been the Negro's and in it he could "be himself." As obvious as the reality of the Negro community is, it is too often overlooked in optimistic analyses of the future of Negro–white relations in the U.S. As E. Franklin Frazier observed,

> From whatever standpoint one may undertake an analysis of the process of desegregation, it is necessary to recognize the existence of a Negro community in the United States with a set of institutions which closely duplicate those in the American community. It is necessary to emphasize this fact because in most discussions of desegregation, there is an implicit assumption that Negroes are merely atomized individuals who have been excluded from full participation in the life of the white society.[32]

The existence of the Negro community is the fundamental factor which causes tokenism to be too little, too late. The individual Negro must not only gain acceptance into the white community but must escape from the Negro community. Integration, whether gradual or immediate, requires that white society come to terms not only with the individual Negro who has escaped, but with the entire Negro community. Acceptance of a handful of exceptional Negroes who have, in effect, "resigned" from the Negro community does not promise to lead automatically to the disappearance of the minority group. This disappearance certainly will not follow if token acceptance becomes a substitute for action to remedy the disadvantages which hold down millions of unexceptional Negroes. Moreover, as has been pointed out before, even the Negro who seems to have escaped still lives in the threatening shadow of the Negro masses.

In the absence of a magic wand waved by some master planner to dissolve the Negro community overnight and redistribute its masses in small increments in white neighborhoods and institutions, the Negro community will continue to constitute a refuge for those many Negroes who are not ready or willing to be valiant, lonely pioneers in the white society.

The Negro church is almost as old as the Negro community itself. While a relatively few Negroes witness to their belief in an unsegregated Christianity by "kneel-ins," services continue unabated in segregated Negro churches which, if anything, grow stronger because of the militancy of some of their members. The central city white church faces the same dilemma as the white neighborhood. For both, becoming interracial is more often than not a prelude to becoming Negro.

As long as school desegregation remains to any extent selective and voluntary, many Negro parents will settle for the half-loaf of education in the separate Negro school for their children rather than expose them to the psychological and even physical hazards of having them "invade" the white schools. And, as Frazier so often pointed out, so long as the Negro community survives there will be Negroes with a vested interest in segregation who will cherish its segregated institutions. So, as this tough-minded observer of the Negro in the United States predicted, "The Negro community will only 'wither away' slowly and not only form a refuge for the Negro masses but for those middle class Negroes who continue to be identified with Negro institutions within the Negro community." [33]

But, as he pointed out in his famous *Black Bourgeoisie,* while they have profited from the Negro community, some members of the Negro middle class have become increasingly estranged from the Negro masses.[34] Although they may carry on a genteel, legalistic, and, above all, gradual campaign for the elimination of he insulting symbols of segregation, they still derive consolation from living in adequate housing, enjoying private swimming pools, and associating in the rarefied atmosphere of private clubs and Negro "high society." They can derive psychic rewards and some balm for the wounds which segregation inflicts on them as they gain limited access to social realms from which previously they had been excluded solely on the basis of race. A middle-class Negro may win the right to play golf on a municipal course; a Negro doctor may be admitted to the county medical association; or a Negro businessman may gain the privilege of paying a high price for lunch and a pleasant décor in a first class restaurant. But such gains are of remote significance to the unskilled or unemployed Negro who can afford neither golf, adequate medical care, nor a diet above the subsistence level. Segregation of any type of public facility is a visible symbol of all aspects of the inequality of the Negro minority, and as such it is vulnerable to attack. But while the increasingly frequent attacks on this symbol may be "full of sound and fury," they may also "signify nothing" for the Negro masses as long as they are unaccompanied by a vigorous attack on the tangible inequality which segregation has produced. The experience of the Negro masses in northern cities serves as a warning that, even when the "White Only" signs are torn down, a large portion of the Negro community may still be segregated on grounds which ostensibly have no relation to race but subtly and effectively block the "last man on the escalator."

But the lower-class Negro community, becoming more homogeneously lower class as the Negro middle class is able to escape from it, may prove to be more than simply a refuge where the disadvantage may nurse their broken dreams. With disappointment and despair come bitterness, hostility, and reckless aggression. The Negro community is also a reservoir of followers waiting to be mobilized by the new Negro men of power, "conflict leaders" who find their strength not in the ideals or the guilt of white Americans caught in the American Dilemma, not in the approval and the concessions they are able to gain from paternalistic white leaders, but in the frustration, hostility, and need for identity of millions of Negroes. Martin Luther King, Jr., has already been identified as the leader of a nonviolent revolt against the conservative leadership of the NAACP. But King has admitted that while he may, with some effect, still preach nonviolence to his followers, he has given up persuading them to love the white man.[35] Events in Birmingham during the violent days of the spring of 1963 showed that as the number of King's followers increased, so also did the difficulty of keeping their protest nonviolent. Congressman Adam Clayton Powell, attacking white supremacy from his position of power in the Congress, revealed his confidence in the loyalty of the black masses when he predicted that "as long as the crackers attacked him" he would return to Congress indefinitely from an uncritical, segregated Harlem. Finally, the Black Muslims, appealing explicitly to Negroes in the slums and in the prisons, drop all pretense of admiration or love for the white man and frankly identify him as "the white devil."

Working to support this revival of black nationalism is a new force, which originates in the world scene but penetrates the Negro ghetto. This is the rising tide of colored nationalism and, particularly, the emergence of Africa's black nations. Whatever the white man's evaluation of these events, Negroes find in them a new source of "race pride." But this is not the sort of race pride the white man has so long encouraged the Negro to develop, an illogical sort of pride which would let him still look up to the white man. As the preachings of the Black Muslims and the invectives of Powell so clearly reveal, it is a race pride which encourages the Negro to look down on the white man. It is a pride which is not dependent upon the white man's approval and it therefore frees the Negro to hate whites unabashedly. Already we see a growing mood of distrust of all white men, even of white liberals. The danger that America faces is that the desegregation decision of 1954 may prove to be not the beginning of the resolution of "a struggle in the hearts and minds of white Americans" but the opening battle of a race war. The Muslims combine an appeal for division of the society along racial lines with their gospel of contempt for all things white-American. Militant leaders who fight for integration may find that the tactics they must employ and the emotions they must stir up in order to breach the wall of white apathy and the strong points of violent resistance will produce the same consequences. Americans, white and black, may have to endure an ordeal of hatred and conflict before they ever learn to live with each other in peace.

## NOTES

1. Robin M. Williams, Jr., *The Reduction of Intergroup Tensions* (New York: Social Science Research Council, Bull. No. 57, 1947), p. 3.

2. Frank Tannenbaum, *Slave and Citizen* (New York: Alfred A. Knopf, Inc., 1947), p. 121.

3. *Now is the Time* (New York: Dell Publishing Co., Inc., 1955), p. 102.

4. E. U. Essien-Udom, *Black Nationalism* (Chicago: University of Chicago Press, 1962), p. 1.

5. George W. Cable, *The Negro Question,* Arlin Turner, ed. (Garden City, New York: Doubleday Anchor Books, 1958), p. 114.

6. *Cf.* Edgar T. Thompson, "The Plantation: The Physical Basis of Traditional Race Relations," in Edgar T. Thompson, ed., *Race Relations and the Race Problem* (Durham, N.C.: Duke University Press, 1939), pp. 180-219.

7. Blumer, *op. cit.,* pp. 6-7.

8. "Negro Reactions to Minority Group Status" in M. Barron, ed. *American Minorities* (New York: Alfred A. Knopf, Inc., 1957), pp. 193-94.

9. F. F. Lee, "The Race Relations Pattern by Areas of Behavior in a Small New England Town," *American Sociological Review,* 1954, pp. 138-43.

10. *Ibid.,* p. 143.

11. *Ibid.*

12. M. Sherif and C. Sherif, *Groups in Harmony and Tension* (New York: Harper & Row, Publishers, 1953), pp. 79-81.

13. Woodward, *op. cit.,* p. 171.

14. *Ibid.,* pp. 171-72.

15. "Up from Tokenism," *The Reporter,* March 31, 1960, p. 14.

16. Figures for 1910 and 1950 from Donald J. Bogue, *The Population of the United States* (New York: The Free Press of Glencoe, Inc., 1959); for 1960, from U.S. Bureau of the Census, Current Population Reports, Series P-25, "Population Estimates."

17. "New Census Look at Cities and Race," *The Washington Post,* March 26, 1961.

18. "Racial Changes in Metropolitan Areas, 1950-1960," *Social Forces,* 41 (1963), pp. 251-52.

19. "Interracial Housing in the United States," *Phylon* XIX (1958), pp. 14-15.

20. *Slums and Suburbs* (New York: McGraw-Hill Book Co., Inc., 1961), p. 2.

21. U.S. Bureau of the Census, Current Population Reports, "Consumer Income," Series P 60.

22. "The City and the Negro," *Fortune,* March, 1962, p. 91.

23. Conant, *op. cit.,* pp. 33-34.

24. "Explosion Feared by Officials—Cuban Labor Hits Dade's Economy," (AP) *The Tampa Tribune,* March 15, 1963, Section A, p. 1.

25. *Ibid.*

26. *Employment and Earnings,* 8 (June, 1962). Bureau of Labor Statistics, U.S. Department of Labor, Table A, p. 11.

27. "The Post-Industrial Society," Background paper, Liberty Mutual Forum on the Impact of Technological and Social Change, Boston, Mass., June 14, 1962.

28. "Dropouts to Nowhere," *The Reporter,* March 29, 1962, p. 34.

29. *The Negro Potential* (New York: Columbia University Press, 1956), pp. 55-56.

30. *Ibid.,* p. 12.

31. *Amicus Curiae* Brief of the Attorney General of Florida, *loc. cit.,* Table 4, p. 106.

32. "The Negro Middle Class and Desegregation," *Social Problems* 4 (1957), p. 291.

33. *Ibid.,* p. 301.

34. New York: The Free Press of Glencoe, Inc., 1957.

35. As quoted in *Newsweek,* May 6, 1963, p. 28.

# SEVEN

# The Specter
# of Conflict

The prospect is dismal; the need for a solution to the crisis in race relations is desperate. But it is not the function of this volume to suggest a solution, nor even to predict the final outcome of this struggle for status. Honesty compels the sociologist to admit that he cannot see the end of the road of social change; he can only warn of the steep hills and treacherous quagmires just ahead. He can foretell that changes will not come about easily and painlessly. Americans, particularly white Americans, must soon awake to the fact that the crisis in race relations is second in gravity only to the threat of nuclear war. The conclusions and suggestions advanced below are not intended as the details of a comprehensive, integrated plan for the resolution of the crisis. They are, rather, cautions against false trails.

It is true that tokenism is "too little and too late." But it is also true that token desegregation will be the dominant pattern until the cultural deficit of the Negro masses is reduced or the majority of Negroes reject integration as a goal, as the Black Muslims would have it. Although many local laws sustaining compulsory, racial segregation survive pending the day they are specifically challenged, segregation is legally dead. Despite the volume of criticism aimed at the U.S. Supreme Court, there has not been enough unified opposition to lead to nullification by constitutional amendment. And such opposition will never develop as long as the Negro bears the burden of compelling compliance and the white power structure is able to find ways to soften the impact of desegregation through tokenism.

The spatial distribution of the Negro population, the cultural deprivation of the Negro masses, and the social organization of the Negro community make it clear that, in the present circumstances, not many Negroes can benefit directly from the Supreme Court's decisions. Only a minority of "qualified," highly motivated individuals will be willing and able to take advantage of the opportunities provided by the new legal principle. Over and over again it has been demonstrated that plans for "voluntary desegregation" either result in token desegregation or, if more than a token number of Negro volunteers appear, in the eventual "resegregation" of the institution or neighborhood.

To make desegregation compulsory and comprehensive, not voluntary and token, would require major changes in the civil rights laws, in the judicial application of the principle of equity, and in the role of the federal executive. There is little indication that the American electorate to whom the legislative and executive branches are responsive is likely to demand the resolution of the crisis through compulsory desegregation on a massive scale. Ironically, authoritarian methods would be necessary to bring about rapid desegregation and "racial democracy" in the absence of a legislative mandate. But there is great danger that the use of such methods would at once transform the apathy and complacency of the majority of the white populace into active resistance.

## TOKENISM AS A CONTINUING OBJECTIVE

In spite of the increasing volume of denunciations of tokenism by Negro leaders, many of these leaders will continue to fight for the symbolic gains which token desegregation brings. Even tokenism shatters the castelike uniformity of traditional patterns of segregation. It provides the basis of hopes for greater gains in the future. Even Negroes who may not be able to take advantage of token desegregation experience a temporary feeling of victory, although they will soon feel frustrated and impatient again. Getting James Meredith into the University of Mississippi did represent a victory for Negroes, just as failure to keep Autherine Lucy in the University of Alabama constituted a defeat. Negroes will continue to fight for such victories as long as they can—and rejoice in them.

More important, for the Negro leader who cannot accept the "racism in reverse" of the Black Muslims, this is the easiest type of victory to achieve. In spite of the costs and the danger, it is still easier to desegregate a few lunch counters than to raise the level of living of millions of Negroes; to gain the admission of a handful of Negro children to a few white schools than to raise the achievement level of thousands of children still attending segregated schools; to compel the employment of a few white-collar workers in "white" stores than to solve the problem of Negro unemployment. Segregation is the symbol of the pervasive inequality of the Negro in American society, and the symbol is a more accessible target than the basic, underlying inequality. Thus either in response to the pricks of conscience or the desire for prestige, many Negro leaders will continue to lead attacks on the surface manifestations of the Negro's inferior status. They will receive support from many lower-class Negroes, who will derive psychic rewards from the struggle even if the victory brings them no direct gains. They will receive even more enthusiastic support from middle-class Negroes, who are able to take advantage of the gains of token desegregation. Because they are "ready" for desegregation, such middle-class Negroes find the arbitrary racial barriers all the more onerous.

## CONFLICT OVER TOKENISM

But even when Negro leaders accept the limited objective of tokenism, their relationship with white society and its leaders is fundamentally one of conflict. From the legal standpoint, tokenism consists of granting to the individual citizen rights which are his by virtue of his citizenship and which cannot be withheld on the basis of his group membership. They are *his* rights, not the group's. But it is difficult for the white citizen to perceive the Negro pioneer as an individual claimant when he claims rights that have long been enjoyed only by the white group. When the individual is aided and supported by Negro organizations and his legal claim is described as a "class action," it is even more difficult for the white person to see the Negro claimant as anything but a representative and spearhead of the entire Negro community. The Negro pioneer, no matter how exceptional, stands in the shadow of the culturally deprived Negro community. As long as he does, white Americans will react to the threat of having to accept the Negro lower class along with the pioneer. They will not voluntarily sacrifice their status advantage. They will give it up only when confronted with power that threatens other values.

So the prospect is that most of the Negro's gains will continue to come through conflict. White liberals may regard each token step as a gain for which all Americans should be thankful. But in the context of intergroup relations each of these steps will be a victory for Negroes and a defeat for the dominant white group. But such small, symbolic victories will not signify the termination of the power struggle either in the communities in which they occur or in the larger American society. In spite of temporary victories or temporary defeats, the drive of Negroes for identity will continue for a long time. There will be respites following periods of struggle and stress. Token victories will not eliminate the substratum of dissatisfaction which underlies the Negro's struggle, but they will encourage renewal of the struggle.

## REALISTIC AND NONREALISTIC CONFLICT

This analysis suggests another reason for expecting recurrent conflict over a long period. That is the fact that much of the conflict will be "nonrealistic." Coser, on the basis of Simmel's analysis of conflict,[1] distinguishes between "realistic" and "nonrealistic" conflict in this way:

> Conflicts which arise from frustration of specific demands within the relationship and from estimates of gains of the participants, and which are directed at the presumed frustrating object, can be called *realistic conflicts* insofar as they are means towards a specific result. *Nonrealistic conflicts,* on the other hand, although still involving interaction between two or more persons, are not occasioned by the rival ends of the antagonists but by the need for tension relief of at least one of them.[2]

The displacement of hostility by members of the dominant group through aggression toward minority groups has been the subject of extensive analysis. In view of the very realistic character of the status struggle, it has been overemphasized. On the other hand, little research has been directed toward identifying nonrealistic elements in the aggressive acts of the minority group. By definition, the minority group finds in the many forms of discrimination numerous sources of frustration. Ample basis exists, therefore, for realistic conflict initiated by the minority. Nevertheless the most basic and severe frustration which the minority-group member experiences is most diffuse and nonspecific. This is the general status-deprivation and sense of inferiority which he experiences. Although it is relatively easy for him to attack the specific, symbolic manifestations of this status-deprivation, a massive attack on the very structure of the society is necessary for action against the fundamental source of frustration. The social structure is such that the minority group may be prevented from attacking the ultimate source of discrimination and frustration because this source is either too powerful or too inaccessible. For example, one of the greatest deprivations that the Negro minority throughout the United States experiences is the lack of adequate housing. Yet numerous studies of the housing of minority groups show that discrimination in housing is supported by a vast, complex, and sometimes invisible structure ranging from individual realtors, through large home-financing institutions, to some agencies of the federal government itself.

Therefore, in spite of the undeniable existence of a basis for realistic conflicts, the targets of Negro protest activities may be nonrealistic. A second nonrealistic element is introduced, even when conflict has a realistic basis, by the fact that some participants on both sides engage in aggressive action as a means of self-expression rather than of realistic striving toward a goal. Certainly some of the notorious attacks of Negro delinquent gangs on white persons represent such nonrealistic conflict. No matter how realistic the basis for the conflict may be, the presence of such participants maximizes the likelihood of indiscriminate violence. It increases the problem of control by responsible leaders and may change a peaceful demonstration into a bloody riot.

## CONFLICT, POWER, AND FORCE

It is evident that the concept of conflict used here implies something broader than merely "violence" or "force." It includes any form of interaction in which the parties attempt to achieve their objectives by demonstrating that they possess superior power. It might be described simply as "a relationship in which somebody has to lose." Submission, not consensus, is the "pay-off." Power may be manifest as force, as Bierstedt has pointed out, or it may consist of the threat of force—"the ability to employ force, not its actual employment, the ability to apply sanctions, not their actual application." [3] Hence the conflict relationship may range from violence, in which physical force is applied (and sometimes resisted) through the invocation of nonviolent forms of force, such as boycotts, demonstrations and legal sanctions to verbal threats of the use of force. James Baldwin reflects the Negro's perception of race relations as power relations when he declares,

> The sad truth is that whatever modifications have been effected in the social structure of the South since the Reconstruction, and any alleviations of the Negro's lot within it, are due to great and incessant pressure, very little of it indeed from within the South. [4]

What is different now, of course, is that Negroes in the South, as well as in northern cities, are exerting such pressure themselves. With their own power they are confronting the power which has always sustained the status advantage of the white group.

In such a context as this, the establishing of communication between whites and Negroes in no way means that conflict has been terminated. It does not even mean that a minimum of consensus has been reached on the issues involved. It is more likely to signify that the white men of power have found the conflict so costly that they wish to limit it, moving it from the streets, the stores, and the courtroom into the conference room. In actuality the white and the Negro leaders gathered around the conference table do not constitute a biracial team. They are two "truce teams" representing the still antagonistic parties to a conflict. Realism demands that they concentrate not on their points of agreement but on the issues which underlie the conflict. Limitation of the conflict will result from the strategic use of threats and the reciprocal assessment of the balance of power, not from mutual protestations of goodwill under "the rule of charity."

This suggests that communication and negotiation between white and Negro leaders can be effective only if the relationship is recognized as a conflict relationship. The communicators are antagonists, not partners. When the negotiators are freed from the obligation of playing the dual role of arbitrator and antagonist, each is free to state his position clearly, in a way that will preserve his solidarity with the group which he represents. But each is also free, having stated his position, to retreat strategically in the process of negotiation.

An important corollary of this proposition is that such negotiations can be effective only when the Negro community can muster enough power to require white leaders to negotiate. In some communities Negro leaders have demonstrated the improved power position of the Negro minority by invoking economic or political sanctions. Another significant source of Negro power is intervention from the federal level, either by judicial order or executive action. Appeals to the moral sensibilities of the white community through demonstrations are not likely to be effective unless used in combination with these other sources of power. Demands on the white community, unsupported by power, result only in the display of force to show the superior power of the white community, whether under the guise of law or not.

The effectiveness of the white liberal as a member of the white truce teams is limited. He agrees with representatives of the Negro community to an extent that is not typical of the white power leaders. But it is the ability of a negotiator to influence the people whom he represents that is crucial to his success, not his agreement with the opposition. The white liberal is of greatest use in the negotiation process in a role resembling that of an "intelligence officer," who is able to take the role of "the enemy" and interpret the Negroes' position to the other members of the white power structure. He may also be effective as a "liaison agent," who speaks the language of both sides and is trusted by both. In this role he can also be something of a mediator, assessing the relative power positions of the two parties at various stages of the negotiation and summing up the progress that has been made. To play these roles effectively, however, he must remember that he is still a member of the white team and avoid giving the appearance of having "gone over to the enemy."

## AN ALTERNATE APPROACH TO NEGOTIATION

Can an approach which so frankly recognizes the conflict relationship and deliberately exposes the opposed attitudes of the two sides have any integrative effect? Will it not simply widen the rift between the two racial groups? Coser's theoretical analysis of the integrative functions of conflict suggests that recognition of the inevitability of the conflict nexus may not only limit the conflict but have integrative effects for the community. The authors' actual observation of such a relationship between white and Negro leaders in another southern city support this conclusion. The city in which this was observed is much more typically "southern" than is the Florida city in which the biracial committee approach was tried. Its roots go much further back in southern history but, like many other southern cities, it is in the process of shifting from a commercial to an industrial center. Its city officials have explicitly rejected proposals for an official biracial committee, and they have fought a vigorous and highly effective legal delaying action against attempts to desegregate public facilities. Nor has it been able to avoid racial violence. It is one of several southern cities in which nonviolent "sit-ins" were met with violent opposition by segregationist elements in the local population and from surrounding counties.

But it was this violence which provided the impetus for a long process of communication and negotiation. While the Negro demonstrators did not gain an immediate victory, they demonstrated their ability to invoke the sanctions of notoriety upon the community, as national newspapers, radio and television broadcast descriptions of mob violence on the city's main streets. A group of economically powerful white leaders became convinced that this sort of notoriety could be extremely harmful to the city's industrial growth, as the experience of Little Rock had demonstrated. They were also convinced that the Negro community had the power to bring this sort of bad publicity to the city again. As Coser suggests, "Conflict consists in a test of power between antagonistic parties. Accommodation between them is possible only if each is aware of the relative strengths of both parties." [5] In this episode of conflict, these white leaders saw that militant Negroes could be subdued by force but only at a price they did not care to pay.

They did not, however, attempt to form an unofficial biracial committee on which a group of "reasonable" or "moderate" Negro leaders would attempt to speak for the Negro community. Instead, they constituted themselves as a white committee and, through a Negro intergroup relations worker, invited Negro leaders to form a committee of their own. The Negro liaison agent was able to persuade the top officers of a wide range of Negro organizations, including the leaders of the recent demonstrations, to attend an initial meeting with the white leaders. The two groups met in an atmosphere of hostility; no words were minced by either side in condemning the other for its "extremism." But a sufficient number of the white leaders were convinced of the power and determination of the Negro leaders, and a sufficient number of the Negro leaders were impressed by the willingness of even conservative white leaders to listen to them, to allow the negotiations to continue. Within a few months desegregation of some, although not all, of the establishments around which the violence had erupted was accomplished peacefully.

The militant Negro leadership had won. But as so frequently happens in institutional desegregation, it was only a token victory, for only a small proportion of the Negro population profited from the change. One Negro leader declared, "I'm getting ulcers from eating in desegregated restaurants just to prove that they're really desegregated!" The conflict did not end at this point. In fact, many months later a Negro leader would declare to a white leader, "Desegregating eating places is not important—not many Negroes will eat in them; it's creating employment opportunities that is important!" So the negotiations continued.

Token desegregation, creating exceptions to a predominantly segregated pattern, never provides the enduring satisfaction to Negroes that seems in prospect while they are struggling to achieve it. It does not remove the larger, underlying causes of Negro dissatisfaction. Thus each token victory is followed in time by new demands and intensification of the conflict. Moreover, the militant Negro leader cannot long remain a leader if he rests on his laurels after a limited victory. He must define new issues and initiate new struggles.

> Negroes demand of protest leaders constant progress. The combination of long-standing discontent and a new-found belief in the possibility of change produces a constant state of tension and aggressiveness in the Negro community. But this discontent is vague and diffuse, not specific; the masses do not define the issues around which action shall revolve. This the leader must do.[6]

So, over a period of two years, Negro leaders in this southern city have selected new issues and marshaled their forces for more demonstrations. During this period, however, they have found the committee of white leaders insisting upon a confrontation over the conference table at the first hint of "trouble." Using the language of the international Cold War, some of the white leaders have described these as "eyeball to eyeball" conferences. The results have varied. The Negroes have sometimes won most of their demands, as in the case of the desegregation of additional eating places. Always agreements reached have been effective because the white leaders are sufficiently high in the power structure to influence business men. Equally important, they represent enough power to cause city officials to be as alert in preventing breaches of the peace by white segregationists as in breaking up demonstrations by Negroes. In all of these settlements, the superordinate goal has been "keeping the peace" and avoiding notoriety.

In the case of some demands, such as the insistence that by certain dates Negroes should be employed as sales persons in specific stores, the white leaders have taken the position that they could not or would not accede. They have made it plain that if the Negro leaders carried out their threatened demonstrations, they would use their power to stop the demonstrations through police action and economic reprisals, even at the risk of open conflict. As a result, compromise settlements have been made or the Negroes have shifted their attention to other issues. This has not been merely because the Negro leaders were afraid of arrests and violence. They were even more afraid of losing the concessions they had already won.

It must be emphasized that if this is a committee of white "moderates," they are "moderate segregationists." They have never initiated action to bring about any desegregation except in response to pressure from the Negro community. They make it quite clear that, in their roles as members of the committee, they are only incidentally concerned with segregation as a moral issue. Their primary concern is the image of the community as it affects their economic interests. In meeting with their Negro counterparts, all realize that they are assessing their current power position in a continuing conflict relationship. As a result, there is no resentment of the fact that each group habitually holds a "council of war" before confronting the other. This is expected; in fact, the white leaders urge the Negroes to be sure that all the Negro leaders who might take action with reference to the issue at hand either be represented at the conference or consulted beforehand.

This illustrates another function of conflict which Coser suggests. He proposes,

In view of the advantages of unified organization for purposes of winning the conflict, it might be supposed that each party would strongly desire the absence of unity in the opposing party. Yet this is not always true. If a relative balance of forces exists between the two parties, a unified party prefers a unified opponent.[7]

These white leaders understand that an agreement reached with a segment of a disunited Negro leadership group may be nullified quickly by other segments of the group. The effectiveness of this approach, from the standpoint of the white leaders, was clearly demonstrated when the Negro group pressured one of its most militant members who threatened to violate the terms of agreement accepted by the entire group.

Paradoxically, this interaction within a conflict relationship seems to produce positive changes in the attitudes of the individuals involved. The phenomenon of developing respect for an able antagonist who pursues his objectives with candor, courage, and integrity is not an uncommon one. White Americans may have to learn respect for Negro Americans as opponents before they can accept them as friends and equals.

In a conflict relationship, moreover, stereotypes can be broken down through personal confrontation. Comments of members of these two leadership groups indicate that they have come to perceive previously unnoticed differences in members of the opposite group. They have developed an awareness of the structural restrictions upon the behavior of each side, so that neither appears quite as unreasonable as before. And even in concentrating on their points of disagreement, they have found areas of agreement and likeness.

In this process, which is still going on, neither whites nor Negroes have achieved dramatic victories. In a very real sense, both have won and both have lost. The white leaders have "given in" to some demands for desegregation, as their critics are quick to charge. But they have achieved their goal of protecting the city from notoriety. The Negroes have achieved only token desegregation, but they have done so without going through the costly and painful process of battling on the streets in order to achieve the same result. Both parties have left the "never-never land" of believing that racial conflict in twentieth-century America is temporary and will disappear with the settlement of any single controversy. They realize that conflict in their community is not limited by negotiation it will break forth in the streets.

But this is only one level of the conflict relationship. So far these two "truce teams" have concentrated on symbolic manifestations of the Negro's inferior position, not the underlying problems of educational deficiency, lack of job skills, unemployment, and substandard housing. The truce will endure only if drastic action is taken to alleviate these conditions. Otherwise Negro leaders of the type represented here will increasingly find themselves negotiating about token desegregation for the "black *bourgeoisie*" while the Black Muslims or nationalistic Negro politicians speak for the Negro masses.

## THE PROBLEM OF INEQUALITY

The Black Muslims propose that the Negro in America can solve his problem of identity through segregation, not integration, through becoming fully black and fully proud, not fully American and fully proud. But their program rests also on the assumption that self-imposed segregation must be accompanied by improvement in the material conditions of Negro life. While the Muslim dream of a parallel economy may be unrealistic, there is no doubt that their goal of economic improvement is just as important in attracting and holding followers as are the psychic gratifications of "racism in reverse."

Achievement of identity through the route of desegregation and eventual integration depends, similarly, on raising the level of living of the culturally inferior Negro masses. The white segregationist has long used this cultural inferiority as an excuse for denying even the middle-class Negro full participation. The brutal fact is that it does constitute a real barrier to integration. It limits desegregation to tokenism; it makes the conflict over token desegregation an unending and fruitless one. An assault on segregation unaccompanied by an equally vigorous assault on the cultural deficit can result, at best, in the creation a three-tiered system of stratification in which the Negro middle class is neither white nor black and is rejected by both the white classes and the black masses.

It has been argued here that the struggle over desegregation will continue, no matter how meaningless it may be. But there needs to be an honest recognition by both white and Negro leaders at all levels that segregation is not the only issue, even while desegregation progresses through tokenism. Unless attacked where it is, inequality will still exist in the segregated institutions of the Negro community. Granted that "separate" cannot be "equal," there could be far less inequality even where obdurate separation persists. Granted that segregation may be the primary source of infection, it cannot be adequately treated until the secondary infections are reduced. This is not to suggest a choice between attacking segregation and attacking inequality. Both must be attacked with equal vigor, and in some cases the choice must be made to attack inequality within the framework of segregation. The fact that James Conant, in *Slums and Suburbs,* suggests an anachronistic vocational emphasis for the *de facto* segregated Negro schools does not vitiate his appeal to improve the quality of education in these schools. Similarly, the drive to develop open-occupancy standards in white neighborhoods should be a supplement to the development of better-quality housing and greater opportunities for home ownership for Negroes, even in segregated neighborhoods. The campaign to eliminate job discrimination against qualified Negroes will have little meaning unless a special effort is made to provide training in the necessary skills.

Since the wealth of the nation is concentrated in the hands of the white population, such a program would demand sacrifice by white Americans. It would require allocation of a disproportionate share of tax money to improve publicly supported institutions for Negroes. It would entail the taking of greater risks by white businessmen who would venture to serve the Negro market. It might even require that more white people serve as teachers to Negroes, like the "Yankee missionaries" of the early days of Negro education in the South. It would require the sort of financial sacrifice that foreign aid programs require; the sort of capitalistic enterprise that expansion into foreign markets demands; and the kind of intensive training that is given Peace Corps members to enable them to work effectively with people of other cultures. It is time for America to face the implications of the fact that it has a "backward nation" within its own boundaries, a nation that requires help from its own fellow citizens if it is to remain psychologically and culturally a part of the greater nation to which it still desperately wants to belong.

Fortunately this "backward nation" is capable of self-help, and it has leaders who are at home and wield some influence in the high

st levels of general American society. Many Negro leaders, including
Martin Luther King, Whitney Young, of the Urban League, and
Carl Rowan, have proclaimed, in one way or another, that equality
will never be handed to Negro Americans on a silver platter. They
must fight for it, and they must at the same time earn it. Indeed,
were equality, material or social, extended to the Negro by be-
nevolent white men without a corresponding outreach by the Negro
himself, it is doubtful that the Negro would achieve the pride which
he seeks. Ironically, it is only the National Urban League, traditionally regarded as one of the most conservative of Negro associations,
which matches the Black Muslims in emphasizing the theme of self-
improvement for Negroes. But Young, the League's executive director, emphasizes to white leaders that if they do not aid the Urban
League in its self-help program they may have to deal with the
hatred of the Muslims. For Negro leaders to preach self-improvement to their followers without receiving the aid of the wealthier,
more powerful white community can lead only to more frustration
and more conflict. Both white and Negro leaders would do well to
heed the warning of James Baldwin, when he speaks of the Muslim
argument and "evidence" that American professions of democracy
have never been even remotely sincere:

> Unless one supposes that the idea of black supremacy has virtues
> denied to the idea of white supremacy, one cannot possibly accept
> the deadly conclusions a Muslim draws from this evidence. On the
> other hand, it is quite impossible to argue with a Muslim concerning
> the actual state of Negroes in this country—the truth, after all, is
> the truth.[8]

## THE SPECTER OF CONFLICT

But why should the white American, particularly the segregationist, help the Negro to achieve greater equality when inequality
one of the major bulwarks against integration? Here the American
creed and the dream of government by consensus, not by force, become relevant. It has become painfully evident in the past few years
that, unless the nation begins to take longer strides on the first mile
of the long road to equality and integration, the Negro revolt will
change from a nonviolent to a violent one. The white community
will have to fight those Negroes who have too much spirit to submit

any longer, and it will have to support with its charity those who are too apathetic to fight. The only other alternative will be increasingly repressive measures which would change the nature of the Republic and destroy the image of American democracy in the eyes of the world. There is no easy way out. The battle has been joined. The question is whether the conflict will rend American society irreparably or draw its racially separated parts together in some yet unforeseeable future.

## NOTES

1. Georg Simmel, *Conflict,* trans. by Kurt H. Wolff (New York: The Free Press of Glencoe, Inc., 1955).

2. Coser, *op. cit.,* p. 49.

3. Robert Bierstedt, "An Analysis of Social Power," *American Sociological Review,* 15 (1950), p. 733.

4. James Baldwin, *Nobody Knows My Name* (New York: A Delta Book, Dell Publishing Co., 1961), p. 119.

5. Coser, *op. cit.,* p. 137.

6. Lewis M. Killian, "Leadership in the Desegregation Crisis: An Institutional Analysis," in Muzafer Sherif, ed., *Intergroup Relations and Leadership* (New York: John Wiley and Sons, Inc., 1962), p. 159.

7. Coser, *op. cit.,* p. 132.

8. Baldwin, *op. cit.,* p. 76.

# The Eyewitness Accounts of American History Series

This book may be kept

# FOURTEEN DAYS

A fine will be charged for each day the book
is kept over time.

| | | | |
|---|---|---|---|
| JAN 27 '71 | | | |
| APR 30 '75 | | | |
| APR 26 '77 | | | |
| FEB 11 1993 | | | |
| FEB 27 1992 | | | |
| | | | |
| | | | |
| | | | |
| | | | |
| | | | |
| | | | |
| | | | |
| | | | |
| | | | |
| | | | |
| | | | |